The Mindful Living series

Mindful Parenting

Also by Oli Doyle

Mindfulness Plain & Simple
Mindfulness for Life
Mindful Relationships
Mindfulness at Work

Mindful Parenting

Find Peace and Joy Through

Stress-free, Conscious Parenting

Oli Doyle

This edition first published in Great Britain in 2017
by Orion
an imprint of the Orion Publishing Group Ltd
Carmelite House, 50 Victoria Embankment,
London, EC4Y 0DZ
An Hachette UK Company

1 3 5 7 9 10 8 6 4 2

A CIP catalogue record for this book
is available from the British Library.

Paperback ISBN: 978 1 4091 6742 6

Printed and bound by CPI Group (UK), Ltd, Croydon, CR0 4YY

www.orionbooks.co.uk

To you, whoever you are, who seeks light
in the apparent darkness.

Acknowledgements

Gratitude beyond measure to my teachers along the path; Nirgun John, Ekai Korematsu Osho, Byron Katie and Eckhart Tolle, and to all who laid the foundation for them, I can never express my thanks.

Thanks eternally to Ren, Liam, Freya and Ezra, you're all just perfectly mad and I love it. Thanks to Mum and Dad, and to Phil and Abby for all that you do, and all that you have done, it means a lot.

A humble bow to my mindfulness family all over the world who keep in touch and share the journey with me, thank you for walking this path together.

By day, I get to practise all this with Kate, Karen, Jaz, Kris, Anne, Gabby (Gabs), Sue and Lou, and I miss practising it with Danny and Jess. You guys are the best, thank you forever.

It takes a village (almost) to write a book. Thanks to Jill and Sarah from Orion for all your help and support, none of this happens without you. Thanks to Jane from Graham Maw Christie, agent of the century and great value.

And finally, thanks to *you,* for being ready to change your world. I'm right here to help, whatever you need.

Contents

Introduction   xi

Week 1: Parenting Right Now   **1**

Week 2: Delightedness   **25**

Week 3: Letting Go   **50**

Week 4: Open-minded Parenting   **73**

Week 5: Flow   **97**

Week 6: It's All About You   **122**

Conclusion   144

Introduction

Mindfulness, the art of living in the present moment, of moving from being lost in thought to being engaged in experience, is becoming increasingly popular, and for good reason. As countless people discover the amazing transformation that is possible when you stop taking thoughts so seriously, this way of living is unavoidably and rapidly starting to spread.

And with that spread, it is inevitable that an interest arises in the use of mindfulness in different areas of life: at work, in relationships and in parenting, to name a few. So you may be expecting this book to be a guide to parenting mindfully, to using the skills of mindfulness to become a zen parent, calm in the face of chaos and peaceful through even the wildest tantrum. But you would be wrong.

There are plenty of books like this on the market, and some are no doubt very good, but *Mindful Parenting* has a slightly different focus, and it's not to make your life better.

Ultimately, human beings have the world upside down. We believe that the actions we take and the changes we make are supposed to make our lives better. This is backwards. I know what you're thinking: 'Why would I do something if it *isn't* going to make my life better? What would be the point?'

So, before you put this book down to email me (feel free to do this as you read this book at oli@peacethroughmindfulness. com.au), allow me to explain.

The purpose of your learning and experience is not to make life easier, but to wake you up to the truth of who you really are. You are not who you think you are, and every daily act of living is there to help you realise this.

This is what inspired me to create the *Mindful Living* series; I wanted to turn mindfulness on its head. So, instead of showing you how to use mindfulness to live well in a variety of situations (in this case, parenting), this series will show you how to use your life experiences to bring you into a deep state of mindfulness.

Mindful Parenting is not about how to use mindfulness to become a better parent, it is about how to use parenting to deepen your mindfulness practice. Of course, living from this state of alertness and presence will quite naturally make you a more peaceful and skilful parent, so you get the best of both worlds.

But changing the end goal from parental perfection to becoming more present will make a subtle but powerful shift. It will turn your struggles, failures and upsets, as you travel this bumpy road, from disasters to opportunities. And as you discover every old thinking pattern, every unhelpful belief and every way you are stuck, the light of awareness will become your friend, illuminating every corner of your unconscious mind. What fun!

Parenting is perhaps the best way to be challenged, and through the teachings, stories and activities that follow, you will find the tools to make use of these challenges, turning them into compost with which to grow your garden.

How to use this book

There is no 'right' way to learn mindfulness, and likewise this book can be used in any way you choose. *Mindful Parenting* is designed to be a six-week course for busy parents, and so it is broken into six chapters, with a new topic each day. Every day also contains a mindfulness activity to help you to put into practice the skills you read about, and this is essential if you want mindfulness to change your life.

While you can work through the chapters over six weeks, you can equally switch between days and weeks in whatever way feels right for you. There is no progression from beginner to advanced teachings, and every day's activity is equal, so feel free to try out the activities that resonate with you and to leave those that don't, for now. Later, you may find that the time is right for an activity that you didn't want to do earlier.

Finally, I would encourage you, if you want to experience the benefits mindfulness can bring, such as feeling happier and more peaceful, or dealing with stressful situations more effectively, to do a little mindfulness every day. To assist you with this, I have a podcast on iTunes and free apps for iPhone and Android (all called 'Mindfulness With Oli Doyle') with hundreds of classes in them, and at the time of writing there is also a closed Facebook group – called 'Mindfulness

With Oli Doyle' – for friends who want support along the way, and who want to support others. And feel free to email me – oli@peacethroughmindfulness.com.au – with any questions along the way.

So, without further ado, let's begin this journey together with a hearty smile and a bear hug. Thank you for joining me on the path, and for bringing a little more peace into this world.

Yours,
Oli Doyle

WEEK 1

Parenting Right Now

Welcome to the beginning of this journey of discovery. As we begin this week together, we will explore what it means to parent in the present moment and, more importantly, how to do this in practice. This week, you will discover how to be present and mindful in your parenting, while still taking care of the daily necessities of family life. You will also learn how to bring a spirit of playfulness and curiosity into your life as a parent.

The activities may seem simple, too simple even, but rest assured that they will require your full attention, your complete awareness, otherwise you will be lost in the mind. So, let's begin the week by putting down our belief in what is best and stepping into the unknowing space of this instant.

Day 1: Teaching This Instant

As parents, the unspoken rule is that it matters most how our kids turn out. Will he be a rocket scientist? Will she find a cure for cancer? And, lurking underneath those positive hopes are what I sometimes call 'fears from the flip side', which are the dark tails to your mind's hopeful heads. Will he end up like his grandpa? Will she have anxiety like me? And what if he/she turns out to be rude, disrespectful and unkind?

The problem with all of this is that it is happening in the future, which means that it isn't happening at all! You see, if you look for the future, you will discover that it only exists as a thought in your head! That is to say, there is no future, there is only a thought in your mind, which projects some version of the past into the so-called future. But where is it? Have you ever been there? And if not, if it is just a thought, just imagination, then why do we pay so much attention to it?

There is a belief that drives this fascination with the future, and it's important that we uncover this at the start of your journey, lest it cause you problems later on. The belief that pushes us to focus on the so-called future is that if we don't, then things will turn out badly. We believe that we need to plan, to think ahead and to make the future a priority, otherwise we won't succeed! Let me pull this apart a bit more: your mind believes that thinking about something else (rather than concentrating on what you are doing) will make you successful. Being distracted will lead you to brilliance.

As parents, this leads to future-focused parenting, through which we're striving to get ourselves and our kids to some better future. Recall a few things you have done 'for their own good', so that they grow up to be good people, and you will see what I mean. Ends are supposed to justify means here. It's OK to yell, to threaten, to be mean, if it teaches them to be a good person.

But how are our children supposed to learn to be kind from someone who is yelling or holding power over them? Who will teach them compassion if we are showing the opposite? This behaviour is well intentioned, but it is insane, and there is another way.

I call it 'Teaching This Instant', and it is a simple, freeing way to approach what people usually call 'discipline'. That word has become synonymous with a clip around the ear, but it is derived from the word 'disciple', which means that the child is our student, and we teach through our actions. Teaching this instant means that we do our best to help the child to work the problem out now. We don't say: 'If you keep doing that you'll grow up lonely and miserable'; we don't say: 'You've been doing that all week, I've had enough!' We just help them to figure it out right now. Here is an example of what I mean . . .

Activity – Teaching This Instant

Recall a time this week when you did something that was future-focused when it came to teaching your child. Maybe you gave them a lecture about picking up after themselves or being nice to their sister. Maybe you pushed them to practise the piano because, by their age, Mozart was already writing symphonies. However petty or grand the future hope behind this action, recognise what it was. How did you hope their future would be better through this learning?

Now take yourself back to the start of the lecture, or whatever it was. Imagine that your only hope was to help your child to learn something right now, to sort through the problem they were having. Imagine that you just wanted to be there as a helpful guide, leaving the learnings and changes they might make to them. How would you be in that moment? Stay with the situation in your mind and feel the difference between the approaches. Which parent would you prefer to be, and which would you prefer to have?

Regularly, I fall into this trap, and I find myself projecting into this imagined future. It is ridiculous to project what my six-year-old's life will be like if he still behaves in the same way when he's twenty-four. It's as mad as worrying about your seven-month-old still crawling when they are fifty, and yet it happens! But since I started to focus on 'Teaching This Instant', life as a parent has radically changed. I trust their journey and respect the limits of my role in it. My first job is to be present, to be alert, here and now, and that is for my own sake. From that place, I can help them to navigate the challenges of life, but the future is no longer my business. I guess it never was.

All humans are on a learning journey, and our children are learning fast, so they make lots of what look like mistakes. In fact, they're doing the best they can with the skills, information and beliefs they have, just like us. If you want to step out of the stress of living in their imaginary future and enjoy your time with them now instead, give this practice a try, and notice how it applies to every other area of your life, not just parenting.

Day 2: Learning Timelessness

Today, I want to start with a short summary of the root cause of every problem that any human ever had: they were lost in time, which is to say, lost in their thoughts about the past and the future. Every piece of stress on the planet is caused by this. Right now, you are OK. You are sitting and reading this book, so things must be all right. You may be in debt – that's a future problem. You may have made a mistake yesterday – that's a past problem. What problem is there this very instant? Not in one second or one second ago, but this instant? Email me at oli@peacethroughmindfulness.com.au if you find one. I bet you can't.

The reason I want to start with this is that every day in homes around the world, parents are passing this basic dysfunction on to their children. We are handing down the belief that time is important, that the past and future are real, and that thinking about them is important. It seems that this stresses children unnecessarily, making them more difficult to live with at the same time. It also appears that, in this area, our children know better than we do.

If children had more power, and adults had less, this problem could end right now, because our children are capable of teaching us how to live in presence, in connectedness with this moment, because it is their natural state. And today, I hope that you will allow your children to draw you into this wonderful way of living, instant by instant.

If you have spent time with small children, you may have noticed that they live entirely in the now. The concept of tomorrow (and it only exists as a concept) has very little meaning for them, and what matters most is what they are doing this instant. As children grow, we school them in the ways of time-based living, from putting things off until tomorrow to bringing up things that happened yesterday. Even the concepts of Christmas and birthdays are time-bound. If you pay close attention to your experience on Christmas Day, it is no different from any other moment, apart from the story you tell about it. Now I am not suggesting that we should not let children enjoy Christmas or birthdays or any other days that have significance in your family, I am merely illustrating some of the ways in which we share our delusions with our children.

We can still use practical time to help children to learn about planning, saving, brushing their teeth, etc., but we can also allow them to bring us into a state of presence when we don't need to use time for anything practical.

Activity – Learning Timelessness

Today I invite you to notice all the ways that thinking about the past and the future creep into your life (and your parenting) and take your attention away from now. Are you stressed in the morning while you get the kids ready for school? Notice how your attention goes to thoughts about the future and feel the result. Are you dwelling on something your child said or did hours or days after the event? Feel what it is like to cling to that memory and to use it to torture yourself. Pay attention to everything you say, think or do that is past- or future-focused and feel what that way of living is like.

Watch your children, or children in general, and be on the alert for moments when they are completely engaged in what they are doing. I'm not talking about recklessness or disregard for others (which are often driven by trying to get some future result), I am talking about the moments when they are completely concentrating on what they are doing, moments when tomorrow has no meaning. If you can catch them in one of these moments, then just watch for a moment, allowing their state of presence to draw your attention into this instant. Feel the breath in your chest, notice your body, and watch. And when you feel yourself living in the here and now, then go back to your day's activities, but do each one for its own sake, with as much care and attention as you can muster. This is the art of skilful living.

To live skilfully, we must bring together the ability to plan and reflect with the capacity to live in alert awareness, right here and now. And as most of us have quite enough practice in the planning and remembering part, it is the other side that requires our deliberate attention.

It may be that your children have become cultured in the usual way of existence, and that they are as caught up in time as you are (or maybe more so). If this is the case, simply watch children you see in your daily travels, other children in your family, or others you come into contact with. Watch the way they disappear into a drawing, the way they can paint all day with no sense of boredom or impatience. Watch how they express emotions all of a sudden, then let go of them, leaving nothing unprocessed. Look into their eyes and learn how to reconnect with your true self, which is right there when you stop thinking about something else.

While bringing this awareness into everyday life, you can continue to use the concept of time, but it won't create problems for you any more.

Day 3: You're Not a Parent Now

Identity is a key component of the thinking mind, and it is one of the things that keep us completely lost in thought. Of course, identity is a sacred concept for many, but let's take a look at its elements, and how these can become problematic in the field of parenting.

Identity, at its core, is no more than a string of thoughts about yourself, ranging from the universal, like 'I am a woman/man', to the less common, like 'I am a chemical engineer called Susan and I love to eat Thai food'. If you go through everything you describe as 'me', it is generally a thought, either from the past or about the future. 'I am Susan, I have worked here for five years and soon I hope to finish my Masters.' We don't need to argue about whether this story is 'true' or not, we can simply agree that it is based on thoughts, which include memories. We can prove this because if Susan lost her memory at this moment in time, her identity would disappear, for her at least.

If you explore everything that you tell others (and yourself) about you, it is all thoughts, beliefs and opinions. 'I'm no good at chess. My last boss was unfair to me. I have a knack for crossword puzzles.' It's all in our heads!

All of these thoughts can cause problems when we

identify with them (that is, when we believe them to be true) because whenever something contradicts that story, we are likely to feel upset or disorientated. And, if you are anything like me, you will have discovered that life has a knack for throwing up situations that contradict and challenge those firmly held stories.

As a parent, this happens about 50 times a day because, as I have discovered, our children aren't that interested in keeping our stories safe and comfortable. They are, rightly, concerned with the task of living, and often this process doesn't fit into the neat lines the mind creates. Every belief gets challenged, and as a result your entire sense of self can seem threatened. Most people don't realise that this is what's happening; they think their children are not being good! The urge to control, punish and manipulate arises strongly, and for many this becomes the foundation of their relationship with their children. What if we relinquished our identity instead?

This may sound crazy, and your mind might react with fear at the thought of losing something so precious. But don't worry, you will still be you, you just won't be tortured by painful thoughts, or at least not as often! What if, instead of seeing yourself as a parent and adopting a particular way of behaving because of that, you were merely an older human being, there with these smaller (or at least younger) people to help them through life? What if your job was to help them stay safe and learn, without any investment in the outcome, in who they grow up to be? This is the core problem with seeing yourself as a 'parent': you become invested in *your* version of how your child should turn out, and you try to mould them to fit.

Activity – Other People's Children

This activity is one that I stumbled upon in my own life when I noticed something curious. I work with other people's children on a regular basis in my job, and I noticed that those children could throw pretty much any type of behaviour at me and I would stay calm and compassionate. Then, when I got home, I would get upset about 'my children' doing things much less severe, and I wondered, why is it so?

I was making their behaviour a part of my sense of self, imagining that it was a reflection on me. I was being 'your dad' at home, while at work I was just being with other people's children, still helping as best I could, but without a hint of taking anything personally.

When every child (including my child) is somebody else's child, I still want to help them as much as I can. I want to hear them, support them and be there for them, but it becomes their journey, not mine. Of course, it was *always* their journey, but now I am aware of the fact. This is a relief, and I feel calm, peaceful and focused, everything I need to be in order to be the best parent I can.

Close your eyes and remember a time when you parented at less than your best. A time when you lectured, raved, grounded and generally became a tyrant 'for their own good'. I hope you have an example, because I have plenty!

Once you have an example in mind, pinpoint the beliefs that drove that behaviour. What were you afraid of, or angry about in that moment? What belief was contravened by their behaviour? What part of your identity was threatened?

Now imagine if that was somebody else's child. What would you say or do differently without the sense of ownership, of being responsible for that young person's journey? And how would you feel? Take your time with this and be gentle with yourself. The results can be revealing to say the least!

Today, try something simple and revolutionary: try treating your children as if they don't belong to you, but are simply there with you. Be present, aware and caring, and let them take the next step as they see fit. Keep them safe, of course, but drop your identity as a parent, stop treating them as 'my child' and see what happens next.

Day 4: Together This Instant

So much of our time together as a family can be governed by thoughts about the past and the future. Today we will explore what is possible when we make this instant's interaction, and our attention in this moment, more important than where we're heading.

Take a mindful breath and look around. Let thoughts about the past and the future come and go as they will. Focus your attention on this breath, this instant, and be very alert. Listen, feel the sensations in your body and stay here, now. Be mindful.

To be in this state of attention when we are with our children is the greatest gift we can give them. Better than a private school education, better than a shiny car on their birthday; open, alert awareness is the best thing you can give them. Everything else you do for your children is secondary. And the wonderful thing about giving the gift of mindfulness is that you get even more from it than they do. But all of this is easy to forget.

A few days ago, I was at home and was busy, doing some jobs around the house and thinking about the future. I was lucky to get an invitation from my daughter, Freya, to come and jump on the trampoline. Now, Freya is (at the time of writing) three years old, with the sort of fine blonde hair that sticks out all over the place when it comes anywhere near static electricity. So picture me, a thirty-three-year-old (at the time of writing), semi-fit man with no hair, jumping on the trampoline with a little girl with crazy blonde hair. There was nowhere else I was trying to get to, no agenda or future goal. There was nothing but that very instant, watching the girl with crazy hair bob up and down in the sunshine.

My mind would say that I don't have time for such things (unless it's part of a fitness regime). I'm an author (apparently) and I have important work to do, like writing this book! Trampolining is for kids, it says, go and vacuum at least! But really, what is the point of living? The point is to live fully, right now, whatever your mind may say. You can chase the future until the end (and we all know how it ends) or you can be here, now, living. As a parent, you too can let your children guide you (deliberately or accidentally) into this state of peace, and it's easier than you think!

Activity – Instantaneous Parenting

In my books, classes and workshops, I often invite people to test a different way of living, which I call 'Instantaneous Focus'. This simply means making this instant your primary focus.

As a parent, you can live instant by instant too, making this very second the only thing that matters. Have a go at this activity today and see what it is like to spend time with your child in this state. If you won't see your child today, practise it for yourself.

Bring awareness to this one breath, the breath that's happening now, and feel it with as much attention as you can. Feel the sensations, the breath coming in through the nose and mouth, the chest rising and falling. Feel one breath (this one) and then shift your attention to the next breath (also this one).

Look around you and keep feeling your breath. Let it be the silent, background rhythm that keeps you anchored in this moment. Feel yourself breathing and look at, listen to and feel whatever is arising now.

When your child enters your world, keep this instantaneous approach going by feeling yourself breathing and simply listening and looking deeply. What do you notice about them at this moment in time? How do their words sound? What expression is on their face? Take in as much as you can.

Don't try to keep track of these details, just notice them. This isn't a process of trying to remember more about what happens, it is about being mindful now. Let the past go, it's already finished anyway. Forget, for a moment, about the homework they didn't do yesterday, or the ways they broke the rules. Just be with them now instead.

Keep some attention on the breath and the body at all times, and when you get lost in a thought (which you will), come back to reality as soon as you notice that you're daydreaming. See what you notice about your loved ones when you really look at, listen to and appreciate them.

Try this activity today. Then try something even more radical: make this instant the primary focus of your life.

Take care of the things you need to take care of. Plan and remember whatever is necessary, but make breath awareness the undercurrent of your way of living. As you attempt this, notice how powerful the mind seems to be, and feel the difference between a moment of awareness and a moment of imagination. As you may have already discovered, the distance between presence and absence is short, but they are two very different worlds.

Day 5: When Play Happens

For many people, mindfulness and meditation look like serious pursuits that are engaged in by 'spiritual' people. You know the type, they're dour, intense and they don't drink coffee. Maybe they wear a robe and spend their summer break in India, or in a jungle in Thailand. And they're so busy being blissful that they have no time to enjoy themselves.

But if you actually meet people who practise these skills as part of their daily life, be they monks or ordinary folk like us, they laugh a lot. In fact, the whole practice of mindfulness is hilarious when you get down to it. We are practising this seeming technique so that we can remember to be ourselves. When you realise that, and when you see the way you and others behave under the spell of thoughts, it's often pretty funny.

The key connection between mindfulness and play, however, occurs because they are both expressions of the present moment. To laugh, you must be present. To tell a good joke you have to be paying attention, and when you share friendly banter with work colleagues, you have to be on your toes, alert to join in.

With our children, this attitude is immensely helpful, and living with kids big and small can also help us to cultivate this way of living playfully. Let's not be confused here though, 'playing' does not mean getting down and playing a game on the floor, it doesn't mean spending all day outside running around or playing Monopoly. Playfulness is an attitude, it's a way of living in the moment, whether you are engaged in something that seems serious or something seemingly trivial.

In my daily life, I work in the welfare field here in Australia. My colleagues and I come in contact with some horrific stories and we're often supporting people to stay safe, or keep others safe, in high-risk situations. It may be surprising that there is an awful lot of laughter and humour arising all the time in the midst of these often terrible situations. We take the work seriously, we are respectful of our clients, but also there is a lot of playfulness in the office, and we have some fantastic laughs. This makes the work manageable.

Living in this way, there is an intuitive sense of when a more serious approach is required, and even serious times can be approached with some playful humour.

At home too, we have a lot of laughs, some of which the children understand. And whether it's laughing later about your three-year-old delivering a flying head-butt to her big brother or giggling at the funny things that kids (and adults) do, it keeps us sane. We make jokes at bath time, we get attacked by carnivorous tea towels in the kitchen and while we're vacuuming the kids think there is a monster in the house that will eat them if they come too close. None of this looks like 'playing', but it represents an attitude of play, a way of approaching life that is lighthearted.

Playfulness is actually your natural state. You can tell what is natural, what is meant to be, because it feels right. Stress and worry aren't healthy, nor is being serious, and you can know this by feeling what it is like. But if playfulness is natural, then why doesn't everyone live that way? The answer is surprisingly simple: they think too much. Now let me explain the difference between thinking and thought. Thought arises, it is a force of nature. It comes into your mind, whether you want it or not, and then it disappears when it wants to. Thinking is the act of toying with thought, getting lost in it, disappearing into it. Who gets lost? Awareness, you, life, whatever you want to call yourself. You get lost in thought – I call it thinking. Thoughts coming and going cause no problems, in fact they're quite cool, but thinking too much is stressful.

And when you're lost in thought, you can't be aware of the present moment, you can't be alert and present. You can't play in this state, because play is a present moment thing.

Activity – Inviting Play

There are many ways in which you can invite play into your life. You can play a structured game that requires concentration. You can do some high-risk activities that demand attention. Or you can look for opportunities to play right now, no matter what you are doing.

Start by noticing what is happening in the present moment by bringing awareness to your body. Feel your energy moving and keep investing attention in your body. Look around and be totally here now. Now stand up and walk. Feel that, and smile. As you walk and smile you may feel your lungs opening up, your eyes twinkling a little. As that happens, you can actually feel your heart being a little lighter in your chest. I guess that's where the saying comes from.

Stay alert, because this is the key to noticing your own playfulness. You need to be totally here, listening, looking and feeling, interacting with the world in real time. Sit with your children if they are around, and just look, listen and be present with them. Smile. Feel the inner playfulness, the readiness to celebrate the joy of being alive. Fall in love with the present moment.

Take this attitude into your life today, and see what happens. And watch out for thinking, it will try to block you again and again. Don't fight it, just notice it and enjoy.

If you embrace this lighter way of living, you will not only enjoy yourself a whole lot more, but others will enjoy you too. People will want to be near you and your presence will be a blessing in the world.

Day 6: Practical Presence

It might seem, based on what I have described so far, that we need to ignore the everyday demands of life in order to be present moment parents. Nothing could be further from the truth. It is a widely held myth in our society that all kinds of practical action, sensible conduct and bed-making is driven by thinking. We have the impression that everything is planned, and that it is the logical thinking through of action and consequence that keeps us progressing in life.

This assumption is based on a lack of investigation. If you look inside yourself and watch how things happen, you will see this very quickly. Things happen (including us doing things) quite often without any thought beforehand. The mind often creates a story afterwards to explain what happened or what you did, but it doesn't often pre-plan. There is more to be said about this later in the book, but for now I encourage you simply to look into your own experience and see if this is true. Did you plan to scratch your head just then? Did you decide to put your foot on the brake, or did the response arise naturally when you saw the car in front slow down? Don't believe me or your mind. Look inside and discover what is true in your experience.

Let's leave the mind alone for a second and ask a simple question instead. When do you take care of practical things? Do you do it now, or in the future? OK, some things require planning and prearranging, but do you do the planning in the future, or is it now when it happens? Often our attention disappears into thoughts about the future while we are planning, but it is still all arising now: the thoughts, the plans and any action that happens. In actual fact, the now is inescapable – it's always when you live!

This is good news, because we don't need to make a distinction between being present and planning, which is often an important thing to do as a parent. However, there is a way to plan with presence and a way to plan with stress, and today I want to show you how to be at peace as a parent, even when you are planning ahead.

Activity – Planning With Presence

At the moment, in my house, we are expecting child number three in a few weeks (so if the quality of writing deteriorates in the next chapter you will understand why). This has involved pre-planning a few things, like new car seats, bunks for Liam and Freya, and so on. For me, this process doesn't bring with it any anxiety because it's simple. Get the information now, then wait and see what seems to be the best decision. Once what seems to be the best one emerges, take action if you need to and then go back to what you were doing, all with awareness and attention. For me, there is no chance of making a 'wrong' decision, because the one we make is right at that moment. If the bunks break or the car seats don't fit, we deal with it when it happens. Simple.

At other times, there doesn't seem to be enough information to make a decision. Maybe there are two good options, or no good options, and still a decision is needed. In that situation, I recommend the following:

1 Step back from the information and take a few mindful breaths. Let the information be processed naturally, rather than stewing on it, and allow some time for it to be digested.
2 If you need to pick now, but can't decide, just pick one, then let it go.
3 If you don't need to decide yet, let the decision evolve on its own, and enjoy your life in the meantime.

This may seem overly simple, but in fact it is all you need to make any decision. Whatever you decide to do, you will learn something, grow and be fine, whatever your mind says about it. But imagine if you could take all that time weighing things up, evaluating and debating with yourself and be present within that process. Let the mind chew it over, let the information be processed, and enjoy every second.

Practical presence is as simple as that. Plan with presence, then do whatever you decide with presence too. This is far more sensible than the usual thought-based approach, in which people are often so busy thinking about what comes next that they don't pay attention to what they're doing now. This is why it surprises me that people think that being successful in everyday life is not compatible with mindfulness. When you act with care and attention, the quality of every action you take, from bathing your baby to listening to your angry teenager, is increased. And high-quality actions, taken in the proper order, one after another, are a pretty good recipe for success.

It's hard to argue that being distracted, thinking about something else, is useful in any way as a parent. But don't take my word for it. Notice the difference between the high-quality interactions you have when you pay attention and the distracted interactions that take place when you're busy thinking about something else. The results may surprise you.

Day 7: A Day of Mindfulness

Every day as a parent and as a person, the world comes at you. Think about this, talk about that. Make a judgement, defend a belief, be a regular human. Today, I want to invite you into my world, in which there is nowhere to go, just an infinite adventure in awareness – no future, no past, no agenda and no aims, and it's all about me.

Of course, I care deeply about my family, except when I don't, like right now. They're all asleep, so what do they need my care for? That would be merely an idea, a thought in my head that fits with my identity as a nice person. It has nothing to do with them. In fact, my entire existence is for me, and yours is for you, although your mind will not believe it, no way! But my experience (as opposed to my belief) is that my entire existence happens in my awareness. It is all seen through my eyes and heard through my ears. I can never step into your experience or your life, only mine – yet I don't doubt that yours is experienced through your eyes, ears and awareness.

And when, in my view of life, I see someone who seems to need help, I do it without thinking. When they don't seem to, I leave them alone, I trust them to follow their own path. In my world, the aims my mind might have, like becoming an important mindfulness teacher, for example, are totally unimportant. The teaching happens by itself without my deliberate effort; it comes quite naturally when I speak, record and write words I could never predict in advance. Will it make an impact? I don't know. Will it reach anyone? Who knows? Maybe the earth will explode tomorrow, or maybe I will, and that's quite OK with me.

Why would I bother comparing an imagined future with my desires? It only serves to drag energy into something completely useless: thinking too much.

In my world, thought has its proper place. It's a force of nature that is also none of my business, and so no idea belongs to me, even though I might seem to bring it into the world. Even my children aren't mine really. I don't own them. I just got to hang out with them today, and even that is a thought, a memory.

What can you verify as real right this second? What can you be sure of? Your experience of this instant appears to be real, but it is over so quickly, it is so ethereal. The only continuous element in life is the background awareness that watches everything. All else is the birth and transition of different forms of life.

If you don't understand this – good. You're not meant to. Understanding is thinking. You are meant to *experience* this instead. Feel your body. Start with breath, then go deeper, dropping awareness deep into the body. Feel it this instant. Sense yourself as the watcher of everything, the awareness underneath it all. Everything that you can look at, everything that has a form, is either coming or going. Awareness doesn't come or go, it just is, so don't bother looking for it, just notice what is looking.

The only way to know yourself is through this process, and when you do get a taste of this realisation, you will see that every human is the same underneath all the conditioning. Your children are experiencing the world in the same way, through awareness, *as* awareness, even though they have a completely different perspective from you. That is the wonder, the adventure of being alive, and today I recommend that you devote yourself to it.

Activity – Living Now

Today, for 24 hours, see if you can just live now, as awareness, following the direction that life gives you, without needing to plan, judge, evaluate or tell stories. Deal with, experience and celebrate what is happening now, whatever it is. Allow everything to be exactly as it is this instant – it's like that anyway, so why not enjoy?

Whether there be pain, difficulty, rain or sunshine, experience it fully. The universe conspired to put you exactly where you are now, in this exact body, in this exact place, so you can drop the need to know better than life, to know how it *should* be, if only for today.

Make this instant your entire world (actually it always has been) and drop the need to look forward or back even a millisecond. Your mind will do that by itself if it's needed, so relax into this and appreciate it for what it is.

When your children or others ask for some help, or you notice something they seem to need, do what is needed. Keep enjoying, even as you do it. Being a parent is fun after all!

Continue this practice for the rest of the day. Notice the thoughts that come to distract you, and see what changes when you take care of this instant, and let the rest take care of itself.

Your mind will tell you that what I describe is impossible, or that it is dangerous. Don't believe it. Find out for yourself. Test out this different way of living, with the present moment in its proper place: front and centre. You can always go back to the old way (in fact, you will probably do so at times whether you like it or not), so there's no risk, just an opportunity to see what happens if you become a present moment person, and parent. If you put today's lessons and practice into action, you will develop awareness and alertness in everything that you do. When acting out of this mindful state, the quality of what you do increases exponentially and a serene, relaxed quality flows through you. Peaceful, calm and skilful, you can discover within you the type of person this world, and your child, needs.

> ## Week 1: Key Learnings
>
> - Let go of the stress of worrying about your child's future and focus on being with them, and helping them learn.
> - Allow your child to show you the way to live in the present moment. Let them draw you into this instant, away from your troublesome thinking.
> - Use time and thinking for practical matters; use mindful awareness for everything else.
> - Play wholeheartedly with your child and your relationship with them, and with life, will deepen.
> - It is completely possible to bring mindfulness into every activity in your life.

WEEK 2

Delightedness

The stories our society tells us about parenting can be diverse, but often are unhelpful. They range from the story that parents aren't as good as they used to be (there's no discipline any more, you know), to the simplified story that parenting is wonderful and joyful (and if you don't love every second, there must be something wrong with you). This week, we will bring those two seemingly opposite stories together to explore the practice of finding delight, even in the midst of difficulty. I call this practice 'delightedness' and over the next seven days you will learn how to discover and nurture this capacity in yourself, even when things don't seem to go 'right'.

Before we start the week's practice though, I want to be clear about what delightedness is. It isn't a state of feeling delighted about some external event, and it's not a positive story that you tell yourself to keep your spirits up. It is the simple delight in this breath, in the way the fading light still reflects off the keys as I type, of my daughter's angry, screwed-up face when she doesn't get her own way. All of these are expressions of life, equally beautiful and wondrous.

It is only the stories of the mind that categorise these events into 'better' and 'worse', 'good' and 'bad', and all the other labels we attach to the events of our lives.

When we step out of this labelling and learn to appreciate everything as it is, we naturally feel delighted. And this is our practice this week. Let's get started.

Day 1: Delighting in Difficulty

The idea of finding delight in difficulty runs contrary to what your mind probably believes. After all, to feel delight, we need conditions outside us to flow smoothly, to be as they 'should' be. When difficult things happen, it is normal to feel upset, even angry, and to take action to regain control of the situation, especially if the 'situation' is a misbehaving child, right? You couldn't feel delight even then, could you? Actually, it might even help you to feel that way.

The truth, in my experience, is that delight isn't about the world around me doing as I wish, it's not about getting what I want; in fact, it's not about anything! Delight is who I am when I'm fully present and when I allow this instant to be as it is. As I sit here typing, for example, I can do it in two ways. I could sit here believing that writing is hard, and hoping I can get to the end of tonight's work soon, and feeling stressed. Or I can sit and feel my breath, my heartbeat, the dripping tap in the bathroom, and I can enjoy. I can allow this writing to unfold in its own time, allowing it to flow as it wishes. One way causes stress; the other taps me into delight.

As a parent, I have the same options (although sometimes it doesn't feel like a choice!). Tonight, for example, my daughter was keeping herself awake at bedtime. Often, when this happens, my mind tells me that I have work to do and that I don't have time for this! When I believe that story, I feel stressed and sometimes I get annoyed with the situation, because she 'should' go to sleep. Tonight, however, I was struck by the beauty of the situation. What could be better than lying down next to your only daughter and having some quiet time together at the end of the day? And how good is it to have time to sit and follow your breath when you don't usually get time to sit and meditate during the busy daylight hours? In this example, the external situation is the same on both occasions, but my inner experience is completely different. And (in case you were wondering), she got to sleep quicker when I was delighting in the experience.

So, what brings you to delight as a parent? What are the moments, experiences or family rituals that you let yourself enjoy the most? And what pushes your buttons? What are the difficult things you feel you could never enjoy?

Most people love challenges and get bored if things are too easy at work, in sport, or even on the daily crossword. But when it comes to parenting, those same people (that would be you and me) get upset when their children throw a challenging situation at them. Why is this?

In myself, I notice that my mind likes to take ownership of my children, and to see them as reflections of me, rather than being people in their own right. When I fall for this, my son's supermarket tantrum is not a challenge but a crushing failure. I have failed as a parent and as a human being. He has nothing to do with it.

But without that belief (which looks a little strange when you examine it) that what my child does is my responsibility, then the tantrum (or any other difficult situation you care to replace it with) can become a challenge that leads me back to my natural state of delight.

Activity – Enjoying a Challenge

Take out a pen and a piece of paper and write down the worst thing (according to your mind) that your child could (or does) throw at you. Try to pick something that happens fairly regularly, so that you will get a chance to work with it soon, and definitely pick something that usually pushes your buttons.

It may be helpful to use this sentence as a starter (let's imagine your child's name is Ben):

I can't stand it when Ben . . .

Don't worry about why he does it or what you should do about it, just write it down. Here is an example:

I can't stand it when Ben ignores me.

I'm imagining Ben as a teenage boy (you know the ones) who comes home from school every day to greet you with a chorus of grunts, shrugs and 'nothing's. I know plenty of parents who feel they might lose their marbles when their teen does this.

Once you have finished your example, close your eyes and visualise it. Take a minute to remember how that scene usually plays out for you.

Next, I want you to come up with a mindfulness practice you can use during that experience. Maybe you will listen very carefully to every word they say, or feel your breath as you watch, or notice the emotions arising in your body. Whatever you think may be helpful in that situation is fine. Once you have an idea, complete this sentence:

When this happens next, I could . . .

Here is an example for me and Ben:

When this happens next I could listen closely to the silence that is in the room while I breathe and smile.

So, the interaction that used to look like this:

Me: How was your day?

Ben: (Shrugs)

Me: What did you do?

Ben: Nothing.

Me: (Steam rising from my ears) Why won't you talk to me!

Ben: (Shrugs)

Me: Fine! If you won't communicate you can go to your room!

Ben: Whatevs.

Becomes like this:

Me: How was your day?

Ben: (Shrugs)

Me: (Closes eyes and smiles with a zen-like serenity)

Ben: What are you doing?

Me: (Shrugs and continues smiling with the peace that passes all understanding)

Because, of course, Ben is giving me an opportunity to be present, to reconnect with my own inner delight. When I am focused on him and what he 'should' be doing, how he 'should' respond, I am totally lost in thought, and I am having what I call an out of body experience. This is when all your awareness goes out of the body and into thought, and it's not pleasant. Ben is reminding me (perhaps unintentionally) to return to me and to start from there. Thanks, Ben!

If you let them, your children can show you the way back to yourself, which is the greatest gift a person can give. Today, instead of trying to control them, use the opportunities they provide to bring you back into the wonderful present moment.

Day 2: Learning to Enjoy Simple Things

Today is all about learning to enjoy the simple things in family life. Ordinarily, human beings overcomplicate life in general and we make our lives especially complicated when it comes to enjoyment. We've been convinced that enjoyment and happiness need to come from exciting, complex activities, from having a fully scheduled day, when in fact the greatest joy comes from the simplest experiences. When was the last time you enjoyed looking at the clouds moving through the sky, or listened to the birds singing at dusk? For most people, life is becoming more and more complex and as a result we are becoming more and more stressed.

Because we see happiness as something complicated, we can start to put conditions on our happiness. For example, you might believe that in order to be happy you need to raise well-rounded children who can swim, dance, paint, act and recite the works of Shakespeare by heart. What sort of life does this type of belief lead us to, and is it really what our children need? In fact, what our children need from us is not more activity, more stress and more things for us to take them to. What they need is more simple joy.

Simple joy is what you feel when you sit and listen to the rain on the roof, when you play cricket together in the backyard on a summer's afternoon, and when you spend time sitting, drinking a cup of tea together in silence. With small children, this is quite natural, because they live in a state of simple joy most of the time. Small children generally love to sit and play a simple game or read a book together. They can spend hours out hunting for bugs or jumping in and out of the swimming pool, and this natural, simple joy can lead you back to your own true nature, if you let it. But can you? When your child, your niece, your grandson asks you to read that Maisy book for the 17th time today, can you read it as if for the first time, with freshness and attention? This is why children are the best meditation teachers.

With older children, it may be more challenging to find simple joyful activities that they like, especially if their preferred form of entertainment involves a screen. But think about your child's other passions and you will surely find opportunities to spend time together enjoying simplicity. Maybe your son loves to play the guitar, or your daughter loves to kick a football. Or maybe you can introduce a new family activity that wasn't there before. Whatever you decide to do, the key is to participate with a sense of open, curious attention and to allow the activity to bring you into the present moment.

The reason for taking this approach is that, in fact, joy comes from within, not from outside. We normally block that joy with too much thinking, but it is always there nonetheless. All you need to do is to come into the now, and that joy is ready to shine through.

In our house, we play games every night before bed. The kids get to pick what they want to play, and for that 20–30 minutes, we all leave everything else aside and join in. This gives us time to reconnect, sit still together as a family (which is rare in our busy household) and play together. As we sit and play, I try to stay present, watching my breath and being there fully as the games roll on, so it doubles as a little mindful time at the end of the day, although the kids don't know that. They are much better at being present, so they don't need it formalised. They are able to sit and be there fully in the game, without worrying about the clock or about what comes next. What great teachers!

Activity – Simple Joy

Take 15 minutes today and set it aside for simple joy. You may decide to do this with your family if that's possible, or with yourself if not. Choose an activity that doesn't require a lot of thinking and strategising, such as fishing, a card game, some form of sport or art. Don't read a book or watch any screens, as this will draw your attention out of your body and into the story in your head.

Once you have chosen, set an alarm and then forget about the clock. Immerse yourself in the activity, taking in every detail of the experience you are having right this second. Be here, now, fully, and when the time is over, forget about the activity and move on.

Setting time aside for simple joy is a wonderful way to bring more laughter, love and happiness into your day, and your family. If you are able to enjoy simple things, you will start to notice that life is full of simple things, and they can all be enjoyable, if you let them. The challenge is to let go of our grown-up thoughts, ideas and beliefs and to allow those smaller people in our lives draw us into the magic that always surrounds us. If you can pay attention to the simple things, even for a few minutes each day, you will find your experience quickly becoming more peaceful and enjoyable.

But don't take my word for it. Give it a try today and find out for yourself.

Day 3: What's Blocking Your Fun?

Fun is not something that you do, it's not connected to activities themselves, it is an expression of who you are under all that thinking. But if it is an expression of who you are, then why is it absent from so many people's lives? And what gets in the way of it? Today, we will identify the most important fun blockers in your life and find ways to move beyond them. Let's get straight into an activity.

Activity – Fun Blockers

It can seem that life gets in the way of having fun. After all, it's busy, you're trying to get things done (they're important things too!) and you have serious goals to achieve. But let's step back from that for a moment and examine what is important.

Is any goal, any aim more important than enjoying your life? Could anything at all be more important than enjoying life as it unfolds? Of course, there are times when you need to concentrate in order to stay safe or do something well, but most of our goals are about future attainment, not survival. We're sacrificing our life now (which is all we have) for a future goal (which only exists as a thought). But let me be clear: I am not advocating for a free wheelin' society in which everyone 'has fun' without taking care of our everyday lives. We may need to do the dishes, which can be fun. We may need to work, which can be fun. And we may need to change our society radically to save the planet, which could be a lot of fun. We can take care of the seemingly serious business of life with lightheartedness by only tackling the step we are doing right now. Things feel serious when we project the end results into the future, otherwise we are just taking one step with a clear direction and a clearer mind and heart.

All that can get in the way is believing a thought; anything else is possible. So, while focusing on your family life, write down and complete these sentences to identify the thoughts that are blocking your fun:

- I could have more fun if . . .
- I will fully enjoy my life when . . .
- I have to think about the future so that I can . . .
- When everything in my life is sorted out I will . . .
- Today, I would love to . . .

Now take a step back, take a breath and look at your list. These are the beliefs that are getting in the way of you enjoying your life. Notice I said beliefs, not situations, because in reality, it is rarely a situation that is getting in the way. It is almost always your beliefs *about* the situation that are the cause of the problem.

For example, I wrote:

I have to think about the future so that I can figure out what to do next.

It may seem as if the uncertainty in my life is the cause of this habit but, if I'm honest, I have been addicted to thinking about the future for years. Even after many years of mindfulness practice, the habit remains, although it is far less problematic and it consumes a lot less attention than it used to. And when I am thinking about the future, for example thinking about my work day when I'm getting ready in the morning, I feel absent, distracted and I don't have much fun.

On the other hand, when I forget about the day's appointments and am present with my family in the morning, we have a lot of laughs and I really enjoy myself. I still get ready and leave for work on time, but the experience is far more enjoyable. The only difference between these two experiences is where I place my attention. In one, my attention is consumed in pictures of the future. In the other, I am here, now. The difference is small, but the results are worlds apart, literally.

Which statement on your own list holds the most weight, or has the most impact in your life? Start with that statement and ask yourself: is this a universal truth (your mind may say so), or is it a belief, a thought you have been lost in? What would today be like if that thought went on a holiday? What would you do and how would you do it? Write it down again if you like, for example:

If that thought went on a holiday, just for today, I would be completely present and joyful in the mornings, and I would pay more attention to what I'm doing right now.

This is my answer, based on my example above. But what about you? How would your life change today if that thought left you alone?

The point of this exercise is not to try to get rid of the thought. That is impossible. But if you can recognise it as a thought instead of a universal truth, it will lose its power to make you stressed. Try playing around with those thoughts and beliefs today, and see what you discover.

Day 4: Sharing Delight

If a problem shared is a problem halved (which sometimes I think is not quite accurate), then delight shared is delight multiplied. Sit in the theatre watching a hilarious show with 500 other people and you will know what I mean. The atmosphere is electric. As a parent, it is easy to forget to share your joy with your family, especially when thoughts about the past and future clog up your attention.

As parents, we are constantly sharing. We share advice, instruction, time and maybe even food with the little (or not so little) people in our lives. We share money, clothes and all sorts of resources, but perhaps the most valuable thing we can share is our natural joy.

Activity – Finding Joy

Before you can share that joy, you must uncover it, because too much thinking has rendered many of us oblivious to the natural joy that is inside us at all times. Start by closing your eyes and taking attention into your body. Feel your breath coming and going and enjoy that simple, life-sustaining movement.

With each out-breath, allow your shoulders to relax and do a nice big sigh, letting the energy of the out-breath flow into the world around you.

As you sit and breathe, let thoughts come and go, without dragging your attention away. If your attention does wander, then come back to the breath in your chest. If you realise that you have got lost, be glad! You caught yourself as thought was dragging you away, and now you can return to awareness instead. How wonderful.

Allow and enjoy whatever arises in this moment, be it a sensation, an emotion, a thought or a sense perception. Enjoy being present, here and now.

Now open your eyes and stay alert and present. Take a walk around and look at your surroundings. Enjoy the process of looking, walking and breathing without worrying about what it is that you're seeing. Enjoy the process and don't worry about the content. Stay with this practice for as long as you like.

The only true joy is the most fundamental: the joy of being alive. And if you aren't in touch with this joy, then what can you possibly share that is of value? Everything you put out into the world is infused with the energy you feel inside at that moment (watch an angry person talking, for example, and you can almost feel the upset in their words), so we must start with the inner before we can do anything to improve the outer.

Once you are in touch with that inner joy, even a small amount of the time, your family will start to notice it. They may explain it by saying that 'Mum is in a good mood this week', but this is no mood. It is the simple connection with yourself, right this instant. Simple to establish, and hard to maintain, and this is why . . .

I wake up and look at my watch and a thought flashes into my head: 'Oh no, it's eight o'clock already! I have that meeting at nine. Better get moving!'

I rush out to the kitchen, clatter around and throw (literally) some breakfast together. My children come out and make a few plays for my attention, but I'm not here, I'm already there. Who am I meeting with again? And what do I need to bring? Eight thirty already? Oh dear!

Kids are expert attention-getters, so they start fighting and yelling at each other, and it works! Before long we're all arguing, grumping and resisting, and the energy in the house feels bad. All of us are lost in thoughts like: 'He shouldn't do that', 'They should let me get ready' and 'It's not fair!'.

Our collective attention is in the past and the future, but our bodies are here, now. And as long as we stay focused on those stories and on trying to control each other, the situation will be hopeless!

My family life isn't like this very often (thankfully), but I know that many are. The cause is not in the behaviour of anyone, nor in the situation, but in the thoughts we believe in that moment. Here is a different version of the situation above to illustrate my point:

I wake up and look at my watch and a thought flashes into my head: 'Eight already! Better get moving!'

I get up and walk slowly to the kitchen. As I'm carefully

putting breakfast together, I notice a little set of eyes watching me, and I look into those very same eyes. After a hug and a wrestle, I make breakfast for the kids too, and when they argue and shout at each other, I'm calm and focused. There's no past in the discussion, such as: 'You always do this when I'm late' and there's no future either, such as: 'If you don't stop right now I'm going to . . .'. We're just solving a problem now. Simple.

I get out the door at the same time, but as I ride to work I'm not thinking about the drama at home, nor about the meeting at work. In fact, I'm not thinking at all, I'm paying attention instead.

Give this a try today. Pay close attention to your inner state and allow that attention to flow into the interactions you have with others. Come back from thoughts as soon as you notice you're lost, and see how your interactions change. And, more importantly, how does it feel to be a calm, serene person, even when others are losing their heads?

Day 5: Delightful Connection

For many families, life is busy as they move from one thing to the next in the day's routine. For others, it's a bit dull, as everyone does their own thing on their private device or screen, with minimal meaningful family interaction. Today I want to share with you some simple ways to connect with yourself, your family and the world around you.

My friend Emma personifies this wonderfully. She has a seemingly unshakeable sense of serenity that emanates from her very being. She calmly walks the path of life with her children, and she helps them to connect with the world around them. Walking through a forest with Emma is like taking a tour with David Attenborough (maybe I'm exaggerating a bit), as she patiently explains the mysteries of the lives of the plants and animals we come across.

But it's not the knowledge that I notice most deeply, it's the sense of wonder and delight that she shares with her children and friends. Emma could equally be showing us the works of a master painter, or the way the council replaced her drain. It isn't what she shows us that counts, it is the *way* that she shows us.

Being able to notice the trails of ants and the intricacies of the moss growing on a tree might not be your cup of tea, but nonetheless you can connect with yourself, your family and the world.

Activity – Connection

Let's start with the activity we did yesterday, using awareness of body, breath and surroundings to reconnect with ourselves. Once you feel that sense of connection, look outside and notice what you see. Look for that which is simple and wondrous.

Now look at your loved ones, keep breathing and look with curiosity and openness. These creatures you get to share your life with are mysterious too, whatever the mind may say about them. Make contact, be it eye contact or physical contact, and be fully present as you do so.

And finally, when you go out into the world with your loved ones today, draw their attention to the world that surrounds them. Don't judge it, just notice. Here are examples of things I notice now, that I could share with my loved ones:

- As I look out the window, there's a puffy white cloud that's moving very slowly. The cloud is mostly made of the same stuff as me. Isn't that incredible?
- The grass outside is turning to dust in the summer heat. The pattern of green and brown is fascinating.
- Some birdhouses my children painted are on the desk next to me. The patterns of colour, wood tone and texture are quite delightful, when I'm not assessing the quality of the paint job!

If my children were here I might simply say: 'Can you see that cloud? Isn't it amazing?' Or 'Check out the pattern the grass and the dirt makes. What do you think of that?'

These simple questions allow me to connect with them by bringing our shared awareness to the outside world. They also deepen my own mindfulness because I am looking around me for the wonders of the world.

We often get conned into believing that to connect, we must spend 'Quality Time' together, doing fun things we both enjoy, or something like that. In fact, 'Quality Timelessness' is much more effective! You can connect this very instant by getting back in touch with you, then reaching out to your family and exploring the world together. Whether that world is a forest or a city doesn't matter a bit. There is beauty everywhere, and what is important isn't the external, it is the act of paying attention in the first place.

Children especially love this kind of attention, which is

completely open and innocent. It is a state of just looking, without making judgements and comparisons about what you see. Ordinarily, the mind would see that cloud and say, 'If only we could get some rain. It must be terrible to be a farmer at the moment.' And with that, energy evaporates from the looking and is sucked into the thinking process. In the same way, most children are used to getting certain types of attention depending on what they did most recently. If they were 'good' or if they succeeded at some task, they get positive attention, but this is still a poor substitute for what we could call 'pure attention'. This type of attention is not based on thinking, so there is no good or bad, no evaluation of what is seen. Instead we just look, allowing the other to be exactly as they are.

This type of connection is the only true love, in which we love not because of how the other looks, behaves or treats us. The open, curious attention we direct at them is love itself, the very nature of your being. The connection we make through mindfulness has no conditions, and it can happen whether the other person is calm, serene, angry or somewhere in between. We don't ask anything of the other, nor want something in return. The act of paying attention is its own reward!

Connecting in this fashion also requires no time. In fact, you can only do it this very instant! It can't be scheduled, planned or captured, nor does it need to be. But it does require your full attention, which is why you must start with yourself. Once you are fully alert and attentive, those around you may well get drawn into that state. And even if they don't, you can have yourself a wonderful, inspiring and enjoyable day, and what could be better than that?

Day 6: Delighting in Space

As human beings, we are mostly conditioned to notice and celebrate objects in our lives. Objects include physical things, roles (like our occupation and our relationship roles) and activities. Objects could also be described as anything that gives you a sense of identity, like 'my car', 'my job' or 'my appointment'. Objects fill our days, our houses and our awareness, but what is there in between these objects? Space.

Space is what's there in the morning when you get up on Sunday and there's nowhere to be, nothing to do. Space is there when you sit and listen to your child without needing to rush off to the next thing, or move through the day's routine. And space is there when you allow the day to flow, placing more emphasis on the quality of your attention than on the number or quality of activities that you perform as a family.

Without space in our lives, we become stressed and future-focused, moving from one thing to the next in a flurry of activity. We need space to reset, recalibrate and reconnect with ourselves and each other. And, in that space, spontaneous fun begins to arise quite naturally as you become re-energised and enthusiastic about the world around you and within you. Balancing space and objects is key to a balanced family life.

Many modern families (and people in general) have so many objects to take care of – possessions, commitments, desires – that they are left with very little space. What about you? Is your family caught up in a spiral of meaningless activity? Are your days full to the brim with things to do and people to see? Do you have time to just be together and enjoy the simplicity of family life? That's what today is all about.

Activity – Finding Space

Close your eyes for a moment and take a breath. You have been breathing since the moment you were born, but do you know what it's really like? Take your attention to the breath itself and notice how it feels. There is no right or wrong way to breathe. Just be aware of the experience of breathing right here and now.

As you do this, you can also take note of the rhythm of your breathing. You may notice that there is an in-breath and an out-breath, but also that there is a pause between them. Follow your breath for a moment and pay close attention to this pause.

Now use the pause as an opportunity to reset. Feel the in-breath, pause and check if your attention is still focused in the now. Then feel the out-breath and in the pause that follows, check your attention once more. This pause is a moment of space, and if you pay attention to it, embrace it even, you will find your body beginning to relax and your mind starting to settle.

Open your eyes and look around. Notice the space around you, the openness of the room, of the sky. It is this space that allows everything to grow and to be. Without it, nothing could exist.

Now take a piece of paper and a pen. Write the following sentence, adding at least ten common examples of space in your daily life when you are with your family:

There is space in my life when:

Here are some examples of mine:

There is space in my life when:

- I am waiting for my children to come and brush their teeth
- I am waiting for my children to fall asleep at night
- We get stuck in traffic on the way somewhere

The examples that you identify will become your opportunities to reset, even in the midst of activity.

When you look back on the examples you have written down, they may not seem very inspiring. In fact, they may seem to be the source of much of your frustration in day-to-day life. The kids are too slow, there are too many red lights, the queue at the supermarket is too long, or is it? If you look inside in moments of frustration like these, you will notice something interesting: life does what it wants, even if you don't like it. Whether you complain or relax, there is a queue here, a red light there, a dawdling child (or spouse) there. Your inner resistance has exactly zero impact on the outside world (or perhaps it makes it worse), but it robs you of an opportunity to be at peace and to relax.

This may sound a bit mad, but those frustrations can be turned into peace and contentment by making one simple shift: by embracing the opportunity that these pauses provide. Imagine yourself standing waiting for your child to get ready for school. Picture yourself at the door, ready to go and impatiently tapping your foot as your child meanders around, gathering the things they need for the day. Remember how you told yourself you have no time for mindfulness practice? Well, here it is!

Stop tapping your imaginary foot, close your eyes and take a mindful breath. Follow the rhythm of the in-flow and out-flow, and notice what it feels like to stand very still, to just be for a moment. Picture yourself opening your eyes and taking a step outside, watching the clouds roll across the sky and listening to the singing of the birds. Feel your own stillness and allow yourself to sink into this moment, with nowhere to be, nothing to do. Then, simply continue your day with stillness in your heart.

Try this practice over the next few days. Use as many of these spaces as you can to return to your own inner stillness and, as you do so, notice how your experience of each day begins to change.

Day 7: A Day for Delight

Every day in the life of the average human has a purpose. There are goals to get closer to, desires to fulfil, and tasks to complete. Life is serious, and we all have places to go, people to see, so enjoying a whole day without any purpose, without any agenda, would be a waste of time, right?

Many people seem to have this type of attitude, and I sometimes fall for it too. There needs to be a reason to do something, otherwise you are wasting precious time. It can feel strange to do what you feel like doing in the moment, just for the fun of it, and there can even be a strange sort of guilt attached to enjoyment without purpose.

When I use the word 'purpose', I mean doing things with some end in mind, trying to move towards a future that seems preferable to your mind. There is another way to live deliberately, though, which is to make it your aim to live this instant with quality, with full attention. This is truly purposeful living, and it is the only way truly to enjoy life.

You can't enjoy the future because it never arrives. It is always now. This is why the 'normal' way of living, only doing things for a good, logical reason, is so out of balance.

In families, this manifests as the ceaseless march towards the future. When children are young this may be largely about the daily routine, but we may also want them to walk, talk and grow up, and that desire can lead to stress. With older children, we may want them to be mature before they are ready, or we may be heavily focused on their future (doing well at school, getting into university, etc.). We send a clear message to our children when we do this: 'The future is the most important thing, and it's sensible to be stressed if things aren't going as you want them to.' We teach, through our actions, that everything you do should fit into an action plan – well, almost everything.

But today, I invite you to take a step out of your comfort zone and do the opposite: spend a day with no purpose or agenda, do everything for its own sake without needing to justify it. Enjoy being alive.

Of course, I'm not talking about doing things that could harm or upset others in the name of 'fun', nor am I suggesting that you let the dishes pile up and the dog starve for the day. You can still take care of the essentials, but beyond those, make today a day to enjoy.

Make sure that you test this out on a day when you don't have work or too many other commitments, and if it's impossible to free up a whole day, reserve half a day, or at least two hours, to play and have fun.

Start the day with a few mindful breaths, take your attention into your body and allow yourself to relax into the moment. Ask yourself the question: 'How would I live if I didn't have an agenda?' and let the question sit, without needing to answer it. How would you live this instant, this day, if you didn't have a picture of what the future should look like? How would you live if you weren't trying to get somewhere? The following activity will give you some guidance.

Activity – No Purpose, No Problems

What would you do as a family if you knew this was the last day the planet would survive? If you knew that the earth was going to explode at midnight and there was no escape (in other words, if there were no tomorrow), what would you do for the day? Write down three to five simple, do-able things that you would love to do with your family on the Earth's last day. Here is my list:

If there were no tomorrow, I would:

- Take the kids into nature
- Go for a swim
- Go fishing
- Jump on the trampoline
- Go to the park

Take a look at your list and ask your family to join you in one or two of those activities today. If they say no (or if you're by yourself today), then good, you can enjoy it alone. If they say yes, then follow these instructions carefully:

- While you are there, doing the activity, be in it fully. No phones, no tablets and no photos, just do it and enjoy it.
- Don't try to get anywhere through the activity. If you're playing a game together, don't coach your child to improve their skills. Don't try to win or lose, just be totally in the activity.

- When it's over. Leave it behind. Don't try to cling to the activity or the experience, move on to enjoying the next thing.

After you have finished your delightful activities, ask yourself: 'Could I approach everything in my life with this attitude?' Of course, sometimes you need to plan for practical purposes, like getting a meal ready at a particular time, or getting a piece of work in on time. But, knowing the date/time you would like to complete it, why not fully immerse yourself in the doing and see what the results are. I promise that you'll be surprised.

Having spent a day in purposeless awareness, you know how to concentrate on the doing and let the results take care of themselves. As you continue to practise this way of living, you will notice that things get done with ease and efficiency, and that stress melts away as soon as you leave the future in its proper place and make this instant your primary focus.

Week 2: Key Learnings

- Challenges can become very helpful if you embrace them wholeheartedly.
- Use your curiosity to find the joy in simple things.
- Delight is natural! If you aren't experiencing it, take some time to find out what's getting in the way.
- If you *are* experiencing delight in life right now, ask your child some questions to help them to notice it too.
- Embrace the spaces in your day and you will find yourself a whole lot happier.

WEEK 3

Letting Go

With so much pressure on parents these days, the idea of letting go of some of the responsibility, of the seriousness of the role, may seem counterintuitive. If you scan the internet for a minute or two, you will find scores of articles on things you need to pick up, new skills, ideas and knowledge, in order to be a good enough parent. But where does all of this lead us? In my experience, it leads to confusion, it leads to stress and it leads to disconnection. It is confusing to try to remember it all and get it 'right'. It is stressful to try to change someone or to control the way they learn and grow. And when this becomes our approach, disconnection seems inevitable.

So, this week, keep an open mind. You can always pick up the responsibility next week if it all goes wrong, but for only seven days, try being responsible for your *self* instead of your child. Try owning your internal thoughts, feelings and reactions, and allowing your child the space to learn, grow and make mistakes. Let go of the pressure and pick up your natural curiosity instead.

Day 1: Let Go of the Stick
(and the Carrot Too)!

It is a popular belief in Western culture that, without authority figures telling them what to do, children will go astray. They will turn into rabid, savage monsters, incapable of living in a society that needs rules to keep things running smoothly. And, as a parent, it is your job to enforce these rules, and to come up with nice rewards to encourage your children to do the right thing. But does it work?

If we look at the adults who say these kinds of things (that would be us), we will quickly notice that most adults bend the rules, stretch the limits and push the boundaries, and mostly no one cares. Most people are late for work some days, or they leave early (or both). Most people look busy when they're actually web browsing at least once in their lives and most people say or think unkind things, perhaps several times a day. If I had a parent figure watching me all day, I would barely get anything done as I would need to keep stopping for a pep talk roughly every 15 seconds to correct some indiscretion.

So, did we learn from those serious conversations and helpful suggestions our parents made? Or did we learn from watching, observing the behaviour of those around us and finding our own way in the world? Sit with the question for a moment.

Taking it a step further, when you saw the adults in your life telling you to do one thing while you could see them doing another, how did you feel about them? Did you respect and revere them, or did you rebel?

Children are mirror images of us adults. They see how we behave and copy it, otherwise where are they getting it from?

So today, for 24 hours, I invite you to take a 180-degree turn on your discipline journey, and focus on yourself. Start with this powerful exercise.

Activity – Good Advice

Advice is free, easy to find and usually nobody wants it, but today you will actively seek some good advice from the one person who knows you best – *you*.

Take a piece of paper out and write the name of the child in your life who you think needs to change the most (even if they're sixty-five years old). Then write the word 'should' and quickly write down everything they should do differently. My list would look something like this:

Liam should:

- Be kinder
- Be more flexible
- Pick up after himself
- Have more fun
- Grow up a bit

Take a few minutes to write your list.

Now take your pen and cross the person's name out. Put an emphatic line through it like a grumpy old history teacher. In its place, write the most powerful word in our language: 'I'.

So now my list looks like this:

I should:

- Be kinder
- Be more flexible

- Pick up after myself
- Have more fun
- Grow up a bit

Looking at the list, I can see straightaway that there are dozens of ways in which I could take this advice in my everyday life. And if I am not yet living up to my own standards in these areas all the time, then what right have I to tell Liam how to do it? If I ignore his behaviour and pay attention to my own, it will serve us both.

When I see my child as a reflection of myself, my mind wants to go into control mode. Sometimes the image doesn't look the way I want it to and there is an urge to manipulate it, as discussed above. But if I sit quietly and meditate on the things that push my buttons, the behaviours I want to change, and if I look for them in me, they are easy to find.

Does this mean that I can't set limits and keep my children safe? No. But it means that I can come from a position of humility and understanding, that I can be there alongside him, learning how to play this game called life too. We're both learning, both trying to figure it out, and I can still say, 'No', and I can still say, 'You need a shower'.

Both the carrot and the stick are tools of authority. But what teaches is not what children hear but what they see, which is wonderful. Today, smile when you see a chance to take your own advice. Relax and enjoy being with your child. And if something comes up that would have brought out the stick, then try being the model instead, and see how your child responds.

Day 2: Let Them Show You How To Be Yourself

Parenting is an interesting and a demanding business. It simultaneously asks you to be your best while throwing challenges at you that can leave you short on energy, sleep and patience. But the biggest challenge of parenting is that it requires you to know yourself, while pulling your attention away from you to your children.

Attention is energy, and wherever you invest it, there will be growth. If you pay loving attention to your garden, the plants will do well, and it takes the same careful, loving attention to help our children thrive. The problem this can create, however, is that it leaves us living through them. It leaves us without a strong sense of who we are, except as mum, dad or aunty. This imbalance is an extension of the mind's normal method of pursuing happiness: looking outside, but it seems to become intensified for many parents, who feel the pressure to make sure that their child is successful, kind and well adjusted.

And so the attention that flows into parenting is not simple, mindful awareness, it is the judgemental energy of the mind. We analyse, evaluate and calculate the best moves for our children, and then we try to get them moving in the right direction. So attention is not really paid to them, but to thoughts *about* them.

My friend Kaye illustrates this perfectly, because she is the epitome of the 'good mother'. Kaye has spent her life focused on what she thought her children needed, and now her life revolves around caring for grandchildren, babysitting and being ready to drop her own life at a moment's notice to help out. For Kaye, this doesn't come from love, it comes from the fear of not being good enough, of not caring enough. Don't get me wrong, she loves those children and grandchildren, but more than that she feels resentment and fear. Resentment because her life is not hers, and fear because if she lost that role, she would lose her imagined identity. As thoughts about this run circles in Kaye's head, life is difficult, and she suffers a lot.

Being lost in thought is stressful, and as that stress arises, we can see it as a signal that we have invested too much attention in thought, and not enough inside ourselves. If we use this signal as a reminder to return our attention to our inner world, and to start from there, it becomes a great opportunity to find our own inner peace.

Activity – Finding You

Forget about your children for a moment and imagine that your only purpose in life is to be happy. Because you can only be happy now (as this is the only moment that exists), it makes sense to start by bringing your attention into the present moment. What does your body feel like? What is your emotional state? How does the air feel against your skin? Take a few breaths and return your attention to now.

Drop your attention a little deeper into your body and feel your own presence. Can you feel yourself there, the awareness that watches all that unfolds in your world? Breathe and look around as pure awareness, attention that is free from thought. As you feel the breath and look, notice who is aware of breath, who notices what you see. This awareness is who you are.

When you interact with your child today, see if you can stay conscious of this awareness. Try to watch from this place of simplicity, of peace, as your child makes their way in the world. And make that noticing your primary aim, leaving your child free to make their own path with your full support.

As Byron Katie points out in her wonderful book *Loving What Is*, when you are over there in your child's business, mentally living her life for her, and she's there too, it leaves nobody to live *your* life skilfully. But luckily for us, we have our children to help us notice those times when our attention wanders to someone else's life. Mostly, humans then get upset and angry, blaming the other person for the stress they are feeling, but now you have a different path you can take. Instead of getting cranky with your child, you can be grateful that they are there to help you to return to yourself. You can go inside and reconnect with your inner world, and you can regain the peace that was hidden when you were busy pointing fingers. You might even like to thank your child for the accidental reminder. 'When you did that, I felt so angry, and then I remembered it's none of my business. Thank you.' And even if you don't, you can enjoy the wonderful simplicity of a moment or two of mindful awareness.

Day 3: Let Go of Perfection

Parents should be perfect. Everybody knows this is true. And from the helpful onlookers at the supermarket to the condescending parents whose children are just a little bit better than ours, everyone also knows that you aren't quite there.

In a culture of superficial perfection, there is much judgement from others, together with well-meaning advice that can feed our self-doubt. Believing the judgements of others leads many parents to feel like frauds, as if they are going through the motions without any real idea of what they are doing.

More important than those people, your own mind knows well, and in great detail, what is wrong with you as a parent, what you need to do differently and how the future will turn out if you follow its ten-point plan. This is how the mind works, of course. It points out the seeming gaps in this moment and projects a future in which everything is solved. This takes attention away from now and into a world that doesn't exist. It is stressful and it distracts us from paying attention to what we're doing now.

The mind both loves and hates imperfection. It loves having something to think about, talk about and make wrong, and it hates the feeling of not being good enough. For many people, this is what much of their life is made up of: complaints (both inner and outer) and dissatisfaction. Think of a friend or relative who fits into this category; someone who isn't ever quite happy with the way things are and who loves to talk about it. Underneath the complaining (which is often about other people), you will find a deep insecurity, which is covered up temporarily by the process of focusing on the apparent faults of others.

Further below this insecurity, we hurt because we are disconnected from ourselves and because we cannot allow ourselves to be as we are right now. This combination of disconnection and dissatisfaction has sold billions of self-help books over the past few decades, and it fuels much of the mental activity and behaviour of us poor old parents.

After all, your children are seen by the mind as a reflection of you, and if they're not good enough, you aren't either. And, while it's often easy to hide our own shortcomings or explain them away, when we see them reflected in our children, it is very difficult to ignore. Confronted with this difficult situation, many parents focus on becoming perfect, in the hope that, when they attain perfection, the feeling will go away and they will be OK again. There are two levels on which parents may seek perfection, and both are equally problematic. Here they are:

Level 1: I want my children to be perfect

Many parents feel this way deep down, and so they correct, coach, cajole, threaten and wring their hands, wondering if their little darling will become Prime Minister or end up unemployed. These thoughts can enter your mind whether your child is a dribbling bundle of cuteness or if they are forty-five with kids of their own – the mind doesn't differentiate. And so many parents keep coaching and correcting long after it is needed or helpful. They don't know how to relate any other way, and so their interactions become awkward and stilted. Or their children run away when they can, seeking the space to find their own way, out of the glare of the perfectionistic spotlight.

Level 2: I want to be the perfect parent

The second level is just as tricky. Many parents have such high standards for themselves that they seek to be the heroic, perfect parent. This process puts you in the spotlight, as if your child's fortunes rise and fall with your performance from day-to-day, completely independent of what else is happening for them. Seeming glitches in the path, or simple developmental stages, can become sources of anxiety and worry, as they must be a sign that you're not doing it right.

That's correct – you're not doing it right! You'll never do it right according to the mind. The universe will only let your child experience what they're meant to experience, including your so-called mistakes and failures. Are you saying the intelligent universe made a mistake?

And when others seem to be judging you and your child, making out that there is something wrong with them and that it's your fault, the quest for the holy grail of parenting can intensify even further. This robs family life of its joy because it feels like a constant failing in which no one is doing a good enough job, all because we are seeking this idealistic life as parents.

The path of perfectionism can make us stiff and guarded. It can prevent us from opening to the wonderful opportunity that we call failure, and from learning together as we navigate this thing called life. So today, be an 'imperfectionist' instead.

Activity – The Imperfectionist

Being a perfectionist is easy: listen to your mind, read a few parenting books and ask for an agony aunt's advice, then act as if becoming perfect (through yourself or your child) was the most important thing in the world. More important than your happiness, your peace, your enjoyment. Then, just keep going and have a miserable life.

Being an imperfectionist takes far more skill and fortitude, but it starts with a simple commitment: 'Today, I will make a mistake!' Make this promise today, and as you spend time with your loved ones, watch yourself and take note of the times when you speak, act or think in a way that doesn't serve you or your family. When that happens, take a breath and notice what is happening inside you. Make space for the discomfort, the anger, the sadness and the thoughts that accompany the feeling to arise and express themselves. Stay with this until you feel clear once again, then go to your loved one. Tell them about what you learnt, what you felt, and what you'd like to try next time. Relish the so-called mistake and delight in the chance to learn something new about yourself.

Congratulations, you have entered the peaceful, joyful path of the imperfectionist!

Day 4: Let Yourself Connect

Connection. It is a difficult thing to explain, but not feeling connected to ourselves and those around us leads to a sense of internal poverty, a sense of lack. Children highlight this feeling, particularly young children, because they are so young, so open that they continually seek to connect with those they love. Children don't have so many layers of conditioning, of fear between them and the outside world, and so they assume that you are the same, and they seek to connect. If you are not available in that moment, many children will become upset, frustrated or anxious, because they feel as if they are living with aliens.

Talking to friends, a few have been able to describe vividly this feeling of disconnection. One friend told me that she was sure her real family were somewhere else, and that they would be there to pick her up at any moment. Another told me that he felt that his family were aliens, and that his home planet was somewhere friendly, warm and loving, with people he could understand.

And thinking of my own behaviour at times as a parent, I can see how my children must think I'm quite strange. At times I take the world so seriously that I miss out on the simple joys they experience every moment, and as they navigate the world with a moment-to-moment sense of wonder, us adults are sometimes more concerned about the ticking of the clock and the next thing we have to do.

So, how do we connect? And, more importantly, how do we use the challenges of parenting to bring us back to a state of connection? The answer is incredibly simple.

Activity – Reconnecting

True connection doesn't just mean a big hug when you greet someone or a nice card at Christmas. It means being willing to connect when others are at their best and when they are at their worst, especially in the case of children. In fact, this principle applies not only to people but to this present moment, in which there are people, situations and experiences coming and going all the time. If you reject something that happens in the present, you are disconnecting from the moment and from yourself, taking a step into the fog of thinking instead. You will notice a shift in energy from the body to the head, as the stream of thoughts speeds up and the body produces emotions in response.

When this happens today in your interactions with your children, use the stress you experience as a signal to reconnect. First, reconnect with your body, breath and emotions, allowing everything to be exactly as it is. Don't worry about what thoughts come and go, or what emotions are there, just experience it all, and smile at it if you can.

Next I invite you to open your eyes and look around you. Take in the world, *your world*, as it is at this instant. Notice what you can see, hear and feel, and smile at all that too. When you next see your child, or any other loved one, see if you can look at them as they are now, not at the story in your mind. You may be surprised to discover that the old story is a stale, boring version of the wonderful human being you love so dearly. You may also find that this person is intriguingly perfect, even when they seem to be having some trouble with this thing called life. Listen wholeheartedly, be curious and allowful, and feel the sense of connection between you. And take this spirit of connection and allowfulness into the rest of your daily interactions.

Children don't feel the disconnection we feel as humans and they don't cause it. The feeling of being an isolated little person in a big world comes from believing in thought and losing ourselves in the conceptual mind. Children will show you that you are lost, because they have a deep need to connect and they lack some of the social conditioning that keeps this need hidden in adults. And when they show you, through actions or words, that you have disconnected from life itself, you have a wonderful opportunity to come back. Today I invite you to take it.

Day 5: Let Playfulness Arise

You were born with a spirit of play. From the moment your eyes started tracking objects and people, you knew that life was a wonderful game, and as you discovered that your body is yours to use, and that it can walk, make noise and manipulate the world around it, you were delighted.

At school, you looked forward to playing with friends, swinging, jumping and getting covered in mud, and the adults around you knew (hopefully) that it was right, that it was perfect. Then something changed.

There comes a time in the life of the modern Western human when they need to take things seriously. They need to think things through, to plan for their future, and to consider carefully the possible consequences. In adolescence, we rebel against this seriousness. We make fun of the adult world, we undermine it, seeking our own sense of power and individuality as we push the boundaries of the social constructs around us.

And then, mostly, we settle down. We become fully fledged members of the adult world and begin to experience the power that this brings. The power of choice, of self-determination, of being free to bend the rules. Of course this is an over-simplification, and the experience of each stage is different depending on your situation. I acknowledge that there are great power differentials within adult society as well, but my point goes beyond this. When you are a child, the world is infused with a spirit of play and discovery. As an adult, it is more often infused with a sense of duty and purpose. Play becomes seriousness, and life loses its lustre. Today, let's rediscover it together.

Where does seriousness come from? Is it forced upon you from outside? Or is it something you own, accept and even venerate as you grow older? In my experience, it is mostly a choice, although some extreme circumstances may force us to be serious in order to survive. For most of us though, it is a choice. We embrace the adult world and at the same time we attach a sense of importance to the imagined self we call 'me'. I say 'imagined' because this self is no more than a bundle of thoughts; it doesn't exist in the way you imagine it to. This self takes on a sense of seriousness because it gives a sense of status, because it gives a feeling of importance to your existence, and because it gives you a future.

The future doesn't exist, of course. You have never been there and you never will. It's always now, as far as reality is concerned. But the mind loves the *idea* of the future, and the future, my friends, is a very serious business. After all, we sacrifice our present moment happiness in our search for the perfect future, and we would not do that if the future were unimportant. The future must be serious and important for us to make that trade-off, and in turn that leads to hope or anxiety and fear when we spend our time striving towards that better place. Which doesn't exist.

Perhaps when I put it like this, it sounds a little crazy. It is. And I know, your mind is telling you all the reasons why your life will fall apart without a plan, without striving towards the future, but it won't. I promise.

Your children know this, and deep down they know that your way of living, as if the future were more important than now, is insane. And so they want to play, they want to show you that life should be fun, not serious. Let them.

Activity – Just Play

Plan half an hour today to spend with your child. During that time, you are not allowed to talk about the future. You are not allowed to plan what you will do tonight. You are not even allowed to look at the clock. Let your child pick a game or two and play. Allow yourself to disappear completely into the game. Become one with the process. You can talk about anything, as long as it's not a plan, but preferably talk about the game, or about something fun. Don't worry, you can get back to being serious in a minute (if you want to).

Life isn't meant to be serious, and having kids around is a great way to remind yourself of this fact. Your life is meant to be fun *now*, not in ten years after the mortgage is paid off. So keep the payments going, make sure the bills are covered, and then enjoy every instant of your time with your family. Live like this and even so-called chores become a game, even your taxes can be fun. Play is a spirit, not an activity.

Day 6: Letting Go

Perhaps the biggest challenge in the parenting process is that we get caught up in the belief that we are responsible for our children's behaviour. Of course, we have a role to play in guiding, teaching and mentoring, but what happens when we take complete ownership of the actions of our little cherubs? Notice the difference between watching *a child* throw a supermarket tantrum and watching *your child* do the same thing, and you will experience the impact firsthand. When it is *my child,* I feel stressed, upset and embarrassed. When it's somebody else's, I almost chuckle at how ridiculous it looks, give the poor parent a wink of solidarity (the sign that you belong to the club) and keep shopping. That little word 'my' makes all the difference.

What's happening here is intriguing. The mind has attached part of your self-image to the behaviour of that little (or big) person, and if they aren't doing 'the right thing', then it reflects badly on your self-image. So the logical step for the mind to take is to try to change your child's behaviour, through whatever means necessary, and to get things back in control. Here is a radical alternative.

Imagine that your only responsibility was to take care of your *reaction* to the behaviour, not the behaviour itself. What if your job was to reconnect with yourself, work with the feelings that arise and then simply respond to the situation as best you can.

Today I got a good nudge from life, disguised as my six- and three-year-old children, and the example illustrates this point. My children were playing happily in the bath when Liam, my six-year-old son, started to get bossy and controlling, telling his sister Freya how she had to play the game and getting upset when she didn't comply. It was a Sunday night, and everyone was tired. My mind started to react to what was happening with thoughts like: 'He shouldn't do that' and 'He always ruins bath time'. And as my body reacted to these thoughts, I started trying to control him, to change his behaviour, and eventually I asked him to get out of the bath. Interestingly, with every increasing level of control, his behaviour escalated, and by the time he left the room we were both quite annoyed. We also both thought that the annoyance was caused by the other person.

I stopped to take stock and I asked myself: What is my responsibility? What am I on the hook for? His behaviour? Could I even control it if I tried? (It seems not, based on tonight.) What about my own peace, my own happiness? That I can handle. I took a breath and felt what that was like. I sensed my body, allowing the feelings to arise. And I listened. Not to my thoughts about the past, but to the sounds arising now. I felt instantly calmer. I remembered to connect with this instant and I watched as Freya played happily and noticed the silence in the background.

Funnily enough, when Liam and I saw each other again a few minutes later, we had both transformed. He was laughing and so was I, and I apologised for getting annoyed with him earlier. This wasn't a subtly controlling apology, the kind where you say, 'I'm sorry I got annoyed, but please stop doing . . .'. It was a simple statement of my truth: I behaved in a way I don't like, and it feels right to say sorry. And it was done.

Activity – Letting Go

No matter how old your children are (or maybe it's your grandchildren, nieces, nephews, friends), you may notice yourself trying to control them (whether subtly or overtly). Close your eyes now and think of a time recently when you tried to do this. Take yourself back to the time and the place, and try to remember vividly what you were thinking and feeling at the time. Recall what you did to try to influence that person, how they responded and how you felt when your attention was focused outside yourself.

Now imagine yourself in that situation with a difference: your primary job is to be peaceful and happy, your secondary job is to respond to the situation. Feel your breath and your body. Imagine yourself staying present, staying attentive to your inner experience and allowing the other person or people to make their own decisions. And notice what it feels like to be responsible only for your attention, not for anyone else's actions.

Of course, being present does not mean you have to stay and put up with the behaviour. You might remove yourself. You might ask the other very kindly to stop. But whatever you do will arise from a peaceful mind and an open heart, and the other person may well respond differently. And if they don't, at least there will be one peaceful person there, alert and compassionate, ready to help in any way you can.

Day 7: Letting Go of the Journey (and the Destination)

When children are born, they are completely reliant on us. They have no capacity to care for themselves beyond the ability to communicate their needs. As they begin to grow and develop physically and mentally, their level of dependence on adults steadily declines, but as the one who they needed, the one who was their carer, how do you adjust to this? How do you know when to let go, when to step back, and when to let them flap their wings, even though they might fall? And how do you rediscover your own freedom as they move towards independence? That is what today is all about.

The beginning of the parenting journey feels surreal, special and scary for many. These tiny people are so reliant on you, and you are their entire world. This can lead to a misconception that can carry itself through until children are well and truly grown up: the illusion of ownership. As soon as they are born, they become 'my son' or 'my daughter', and as they grow and develop, we can feel a great sense of responsibility for their trajectory, but are those children ever really ours? In the ancient book of wisdom, the *Tao Te Ching*, Lao Tzu says:

> Therefore the Master acts without doing anything and teaches without saying anything. Things arise and she lets them come; things disappear and she lets them go. She has but does not possess, acts but doesn't expect. When her work is done, she forgets it. That is why it lasts forever.

As parents, we can be fooled into thinking we have a share in our child's future success, that we have a say in their decisions, long after we don't have much influence at all. This creates a tension because we have trouble stepping out of the child's way and allowing them to take the steering wheel. We act and we expect, we have and we possess. Lao Tzu's wisdom is as relevant now as in ancient China. Do your work, but don't expect a result; don't take ownership of your child's journey, for it isn't yours to take.

It is incredibly freeing to take responsibility for your own work, your own role as a parent, while letting your child hold the responsibility for their decisions, actions and behaviours. So if my son is screaming and hitting his sister, that's not my responsibility. It *is* my responsibility to move him out of harm's way and help him to calm down. It *is* my responsibility to try to help him think through better ways to deal with problems, but the behaviour itself is nothing to do with me. I can't make him do it and I can't make him stop, but if I am calm and do my own work with clarity, then he will see what peace and kindness looks like.

Activity – Letting Go of the Journey

Let's try an experiment to see what it is like to be free of the need to control our children. Take a pen in hand and write:

I really hope [child's name] will be . . .

Now write a list of your hopes for their future, as many as you can think of in one minute. Maybe your list looks like mine:

I really hope Freya will be:

- successful
- kind
- funny
- smart
- brilliant
- compassionate

Sit with your list for a minute or two, and notice how it feels to hope for this future. See if you can spot the fear that it may not work out, lurking under the surface. Then take your pen and cross out the first sentence, the one that begins, 'I really hope . . .'. Once you have crossed it out, write this sentence instead:

I have noticed that [child's name] is . . .

Now read through your list. After reading each item on the list, close your eyes and bring to mind an example of your child showing that quality. Be a bold, bragging parent and think of examples to prove that every item on the list is already true *now*.

Isn't it wonderful that the destination you wanted to reach is already here, now?

The secret truth is that there is no destination. In fact, even the journey is no more than a story. All you ever have with your child is now, and in this now they will make their own decisions about what they do, about how they live. Your job is to live *your* life well, because it is the only one you are driving. When we put the responsibility in the right place, we can be free to relax, enjoy our children and guide them as best we can. The rest is up to them.

This week has been a journey of release, of letting go of all the parts of life we don't or can't control, and that can feel scary and challenging. But notice, as you go through these challenges in your life, that the only time you can take action is this very instant, while every story of control and of ownership has a past and a future. Be present in your role while it lasts. Then, as Lao Tzu says, forget it and allow it to last forever.

Week 3: Key Learnings

- Fear and bribery are popular parenting tools, but awareness and mindfulness are far more useful.
- If you feel lost in your role as parent, take time to make your own happiness your only priority. Be happy first, be a parent second, and see how this improves your life (and your parenting too!).
- Use curiosity and awareness to replace the perfectionism that can make being a parent feel like a series of failures.
- Drop your expectations, hopes for the future and beliefs and instead take time to play, connect wholeheartedly and allow your child to be who they are, whatever your mind may say.

WEEK 4

Open-minded Parenting

In our culture, parents are seen as authority figures, or as if they should be. We are supposed to set the rules, to know what to do and we are responsible for what our children say and do. If we are unsure on any point, there is a queue of experts ready to step us through the correct procedure that will, if we follow it precisely, get us back on the right track.

In other words, we are meant to know, and if not, to find out.

But when you know in advance what the right course is, your options become limited, and when you know what a child 'should' do, you are in for a rough time when they do the opposite. Having the destination in mind can prevent us from learning along the way, and it can obscure opportunities that arise unexpectedly.

This emphasis on knowing also reduces our potential for learning from experience, which is necessarily messier and more unpredictable than learning from the experts.

And finally, this approach to parenting (and to life) can make us more intellectual, logical and thought-oriented, and less intuitive, mindful and alert as we traverse the muddy valleys of parenthood.

This week is all about the alternative, which I like to call open-minded parenting or don't-know parenting. This approach requires us to leave our preconceived ideas at the door, and to respond to the questions life asks us in the order they arise. It brings us from a position of authority to that of lifelong learner, and it can inspire us to live fully, acting on inspiration right now, whatever the rulebook might say. Let's begin.

Day 1: Not Knowing What's Best

When I became a parent, it was thrilling and a little bit scary. I had spent years pointing out the faults in the parenting styles of people I knew. I had constructed an airtight image of the perfect parent I would be, and I had mentally rehearsed all the big moments. I knew I would be great. But there is something about the sight of a small, helpless infant staring up at you that can erode that sense of confidence and surety in about three seconds.

I am exaggerating a little, but my parenting confidence was based on a very Western notion that having the right knowledge, being an expert (theoretically, anyway), almost guarantees success. And so, I sought out the best knowledge I could find, and when the big moment came, I felt that I knew best. This is the cause of many problems.

When you think that you know best, a couple of interesting things happen. Firstly, your mind and heart become closed. If you already know what is best, then what is the point in learning more, in being curious? Secondly, you become rigid in thought and in body. When you think that you know, you attach your sense of self to the belief that arises, and once the belief and the thought 'me' are intertwined, the belief must be defended, otherwise you feel threatened. And this is what happened to me (and keeps happening). Life challenges my beliefs and I feel the need to defend them.

I thought I knew what parents should be like (gentle, kind and compassionate), and I also thought I knew how children should develop with this kind of parenting (smoothly and easily). So when some normal toddler tantrums came, I felt gutted. This wasn't supposed to happen to *my* children. How could it? And so, at times, I felt resentment towards those little people, who were just learning and being themselves. This was a great opportunity.

As I have continued to use parenting as a mindfulness practice (easily the most powerful practice I have done), I have discovered something powerful, again and again. If I hold on to beliefs that disagree with what is actually happening, I feel tight, annoyed and completely lost in thought. If I allow the present moment to blow those beliefs to bits, I am left free, happy and curious again. Here is how I approach those beliefs these days.

Activity – Not Knowing What's Best

Close your eyes for a few moments and feel yourself breathing. Take your attention to your chest, your shoulders, your nose and mouth, and notice the sensations that come and go. Bring to mind a recent example of your child doing something they 'shouldn't have done', according to your mind. Pick something that you felt upset by, but not traumatised. Relive it in vivid detail and notice how your body reacts. What thoughts arise about what your child should or shouldn't do? And how does your body respond to those beliefs?

Shift your full focus to the feelings themselves, letting go of the images and letting any thoughts come and go without paying them too much attention. Sit and experience the way your body reacts to the challenge to your beliefs.

Now ask yourself a few questions, taking time to sit with each one:

- Do I know what is best for them?
- Do I know what experiences they should have, or what lessons they should learn?
- How would I live my life, and what sort of parent would I be, without beliefs about how *they* should behave?

Sit with each question for a minute or two without needing to answer it. Sit, allow the question to be there, and keep following the rhythm of your breath.

What does it feel like not to need to know the answers to these questions?

We live in a culture that values having the right answers, knowing the information to respond to the question. We fear not knowing because we build a sense of identity through thinking, analysing and knowing. As a parent, you can respond to the challenges to your beliefs that inevitably will arise in two ways: first, you can try to make reality (your child) fit with your perception of what it should be like. This is not much fun for anyone. Second, you can allow the challenges of parenting to break your shell open, and to bring you into the space of curiosity, of not knowing.

Not knowing is not a state of confusion, but of clarity. It is a state in which we observe the present moment directly, experiencing and allowing it to be as it is. This open, spacious awareness is peaceful, clear and alert. It is a great space from which to make decisions, support others and see clearly. Those who think they know are confused. Those who know that they can't know are already free.

Day 2: Learning Through Curiosity

As I watch my three-year-old daughter Freya, I can see the curiosity dripping from her pores. She spins in the bath, doing things my mind would say are dangerous, but to her, it's just a big adventure. She slips and slides, her head goes under and she pops up, laughing and squealing with the fun of it all. Then she tries it again. Who knows what will happen this time?

Spending time with my children is all-consuming, challenging and fun. But more than any of this, it takes me into a space of profound curiosity, if I let it. As Freya spins, my mind spins too, wondering if she will hit her head or need a trip to the hospital. Stepping out of that frightening story, I wonder what it's like to spin like that. How does that feel? Does water get in your ears? Do you feel dizzy? In this way, every experience with my children can spark my natural state of curiosity, and you can let yours loose too.

Do you ever find yourself saying things like, 'Please stop doing that, you'll ...' or 'If you keep saying that to her she will ...'? I certainly do, and when I move into this space of judgement and assured confidence that I can predict the future (despite my less than amazing record of doing so), I stop looking, listening and wondering, and I stop learning too.

To take a small step towards the world of curiosity and lifelong learning, we can use two simple words to open up some space: 'I wonder'. Here is an example of how you can use it to change your world view:

I shout out to my daughter: 'Get down from there. You'll fall!', sure in the belief that if she doesn't get down, she will fall.

As I try to impose that belief on my daughter, who is a noted acrobat in our house, I feel fear and frustration. I try to control her by telling her to get down, although I'm actually trying to control the feelings I am experiencing. This leads to conflict and disconnection, and communicates distrust to my highly skilled, acrobatic daughter.

By making a simple change, and saying: 'I wonder what will happen if you stay up there,' I enter a space of curiosity. I also join in with her world, as she is probably wondering how it will go too. If she is worried or needs some help, she will feel OK to ask, knowing that I trust her judgement. If she falls, we will deal with it, and if she doesn't, that's fine too. I now feel relaxed, calm and peaceful, and more importantly, the result has allowed me to become more present, alert and curious. Isn't parenting wonderful?

Activity – I Wonder

Try it yourself. Bring to mind a dire future prediction that you're sure is true, and change it to an 'I wonder' statement. Notice how it feels to ask the question and sit with the endless possibilities.

Now take a breath and wonder if you will ever breathe again. And when the next breath comes, wonder aloud once more. Will this be the last? Will this? Notice how exciting it is not to believe you know what will happen next, nor what should. Life is much more fun when we are clear that it's a mystery.

Next come back to your statement of certainty, your demand upon reality. Change the start of it to 'I wonder' and see what happens in your body. What is it like to sit in the question, instead of ramming the answer down your throat? That answer is a thought, a story, nothing more. And when you believe it to be true it stops you from experiencing the wondrous mystery of the world you inhabit. No one else in the world sees the world as you do, no one has your unique vision of reality. Isn't that incredible?

Today, as you walk through the world, wonder about everything you see. You need not think 'I wonder' every time you see something, but look with intensity, with curiosity and you will start to see what children see, that reality is very mysterious, whatever the adults may say.

The reason we think we know is that we carry around with us a store of thoughts, memories about things that happened before. Other than a memory, there is no proof of these things as I sit here now. There is no evidence that the sun came up this morning, nor that it is going down now. I see pink, purple and red sky, clouds, a magpie on the roof. And even that is a story, as the word 'magpie' is a memory, something my mum told me when I was a kid.

Can you just look, without needing those labels? Can you see the world as it is, without a story of a past and a future to get in your wonderful way? Try it today, and see if you can taste that mystery.

Day 3: Uncovering Beliefs

Most people don't have beliefs, or at least they don't know they have quite so many. What they have is 'the truth', not a belief. After all, the word 'belief' implies that it's a thought that you believe, not a universal truth. This isn't enough for most people.

When we are so lost in a belief that we see the world through it, we don't really have a belief – it has us! This belief could be as simple as 'children should be seen and not heard', or it could be that 'parents shouldn't yell at their children'. The belief itself doesn't matter so much, but your relationship to it does, because it can make your life into an adventure or into a form of hell.

When we believe something that contradicts what is happening in this instant, the mind rebels, it feels out of control. If, for example, you believe that children should be polite and wait for adults to ask them and your children turn out to be brash, confident and assertive, your belief will come crashing into the reality of now. Your mind will not like this, and it will try its best to cram this moment back into the box it's supposed to fit neatly into. In this example, the now comes in the form of your child, and so he or she needs be silenced, taught to behave, or whatever else, so that your belief can go back into the shadows and hide.

That's the thing about beliefs, they like it best when they can lurk in the background, pulling your little puppet strings as they control your thoughts, words and actions, while you assure yourself that it's not a belief, but the truth. And the wonderful thing about having children, no matter how old, is that they will show you again and again where you are stuck, where there is a belief lurking. This is a wonderful opportunity.

Because, whether beliefs are being challenged by life or hiding in the shadows, they have a great influence on you. If you know this, you can do something about it.

What you can do is not at all complicated, nor is it easy in the moment of challenge, but it can change your entire world. When that belief is challenged, you will probably find your attention drawn to the outside world, to the person who is acting contrary to your belief, and you will try to change them, control them. Control takes many forms, and this could range from yelling and hitting to withdrawing, giving them a cold, hard stare or anything else in between. We've all done it, and I'm sure you know what I'm talking about; you may or may not say it directly but the message is clear: you'd better shape up or there'll be trouble!

This external focus leaves us in a pretty awful place. What we seek to control, we can't, and the thing we can change (ourselves) remains out of focus.

Yesterday, my son got extremely angry during a game of cricket in our backyard. He ran towards his friend, holding his bat aloft like Tom, ready to whack Jerry with a mallet. Then he stopped, sat down and cried. My belief swung into action: 'He can't control his anger, he has a problem, he's going to hurt someone.' His behaviour didn't fit with my mind's model of 'how people should behave', but I could relate to his actions for sure. I have had trouble with anger myself over the years, and throwing a bat or a tennis racket would not have been beyond me at his age. In fact, I might have done worse!

Every challenge is an opportunity, so I took my attention inside and figured out what the beliefs driving my feelings were. I then looked at those beliefs, I just sat with them, breathing and smiling. The fact was that he *didn't* hit anyone. He stopped and dissolved into tears. Maybe he could teach me a thing or two about coming back from the pointy end of anger without losing it completely. Maybe he was the teacher I needed when I was six.

When I was lost in belief, I didn't see this. I saw the need to get his anger under control and put some strategies in place to do this. There are 10,000 books, written by experts, that I could read on this topic and then impose their expertise on him, but when I look with reality in my eyes, he can teach me how to be. How to be vulnerable instead of grumpy. How to be honest about what you're upset about in the moment. How to deal with things on the spot instead of letting them fester. I have so much to learn, if I look properly.

Activity – Clear-eyed Seeing

Now it's your turn. What do you believe your child should do differently? Where do they not meet your expectations? How should they be? When you find some points of tension, notice how your mind wants to leap on them and attack, or develop an action plan to fix them. Sit for a moment with the possibility that they are here to show you where your mind is stuck, and turn your attention around 180 degrees. Breathe with mindfulness and watch those beliefs, observe them, know that they are thoughts arising in your awareness now. Just watch.

Sit with this open, curious attention for a few minutes and let the beliefs be there. They are not a problem; you were just lost in them. Watch out for the mind's attempts to justify them as being 'true' or 'right'. That's just another story. Breathe and watch. Don't think about it.

Now ask yourself if you have any questions you would like to ask your child. Have you any new perspectives on their situation? Can you see where they are coming from? What would you like to tell them? If there's nothing, that's fine, and if there is, you may want to share it.

What I remembered when I did this with the memory of my son's anger is that my happiness is my job, not his. He is not here in my life to fit into the neat box my mind has created, he's here to hold up a mirror to me, to show me where I am caught so that I can unstick myself. When I'm clear on this, I can leave him alone and get on with *my* job, which is all about me.

Day 4: Love Beyond Logic

Love is not what you think it is. We have been taught to believe that it is either a random chemical reaction stirred by hormones or that it is a reasonable, logical affair. Love has rules, according to the mind. I love you, so please don't upset me, leave me, reject me, anger me or do me wrong. This is the bargain. Sign here please.

This is the mind's version of love, a sort of unspoken, unwritten agreement in which both parties have slightly different expectations, some communicated, others not. Children do not love this way.

Children love with wholehearted abandon and they have no rules that they follow. They can love you while telling you they hate you, they can love you while laughing at you and they can love you while they're climbing out of a window to go to that party they're not supposed to go to. They don't think about love as a contract yet, so these actions can be done without breaking the flow of love.

The reality of love is that it is who you are, it is the free flow of your life energy into the world. It doesn't belong to anyone, it can't be given or taken away, and whether you notice it or not, love is your nature. For this reason, children are closer to the truth than us. They haven't thought through and calculated their requirements for giving and receiving love, so they just live it, for better or worse.

Today I invite you to take a step into this crazy, out of control space, and to experience true love, as you did as a kid.

Activity – True Love

Close your eyes and let your breath take your attention into your body. Follow the in- and out-breaths and feel the energy flowing through your body. Concentrate on your hands and feel the slight tingling as energy moves in your body. Now go deeper. Notice who is aware of this energy, who is aware of the breath. Become aware of awareness itself. Can you sense yourself in the background, watching as life unfolds all around and inside you?

Stay connected with this awareness and open your eyes. Notice that you are aware of what you see, hear and feel, and enjoy that looking, listening and feeling. Become so alert and aware that it feels like a great gift to look at this table, that chair, the sun in the sky.

Next, look at a human, or a photo of a human. Sense that awareness as you look, the awareness behind your eyes. Notice how this awareness is there before thought, identity or opinion, and how it does not have judgements of its own, it just watches.

Now ask yourself, what is behind the other person's eyes? Who are they, underneath all their conditioning? Could it be that they too are this simple, clear awareness? Sit with this question, without needing an answer.

When you see your child or children today (whether in real life or as images in your mind), see if you can be aware of the awareness in you as you look. Ask yourself whether they are like you, underneath it all: awareness in disguise. To love is to see that there are no others, just different disguises.

Normally, love is based on behaviour. It's a reciprocal, expected and often predictable commodity. Children throw this into chaos because they don't see the need for such rules. They love you *and* they want that chocolate bar (and they'll scream the supermarket down to get it). They love you *and* they're going to their girlfriend's house for Christmas. This is still love, in fact it's *deeper* love because they are not doing it just to please you or to make you feel OK. They trust you to be OK, they know that you are always OK, and so they can make the best decision for themselves right now.

Watching my children, I can see this so clearly. They don't take it personally if I do something they don't like, and they expect the same. They don't carry it with them all day if I make a mistake, and they expect the same from me. Perhaps it's better to say that it never occurred to them that any other way was possible. Love is unconditional, but that doesn't mean they won't slap their brother when he has their toy.

When we impose adult concepts on to this love, it can seem that they are being abusive, unkind or manipulative, but in truth, they just don't care. They don't care about your contract, they don't care about your expectations, and they don't care if you feel hurt and stressed. That's your problem. If, as adults, we can learn to love with the same gusto, and a little more awareness of others' needs than our children can manage yet, then we can drop the contract, tear up the agreement and find ourselves constantly in love, with ourselves and those we get to spend time with today.

Free yourself of mentally created concepts of love and your world will start to sing.

Day 5: Playing With Possibilities

'In the beginner's mind there are many possibilities,
but in the expert's there are few.' Suzuki Roshi

Today is all about letting go of what you think you know, and stepping into the world of the don't-know mind, as the Zen masters call it. This may sound a bit mysterious and ethereal, but it is quite a clear, simple way of being. Let me explain in detail.

Ordinarily, we look to the mind to tell us what the world is like. We interpret (or the mind interprets for us) the things we see, hear and experience. We then fit the stories we create about these events into our bigger story, which I like to call *The Story of Me*. Researchers in the field of psychology have been able to demonstrate that what we remember and incorporate into that story is a tiny fragment of what we experience, and we instinctively look for and hang on to the details that support our existing stories.

This means that we already know conceptually (through thought) what the world is like, and every new input is fed through the mind's filters and rapidly turned into a story. So, most of what people think of as their experience is actually memory, and not even accurate memory! This is the curse of the expert. They already know what the world is like and so they stop looking, they see few possibilities.

This way of living is all in the head, with brief trips into actual experience when absolutely necessary. The way of present moment living (and parenting) is the opposite: a life of experience with brief trips into the mind when necessary. This is how my children live, and if I let them, they can remind me to take a step in their direction. Here is a practical tool I have discovered for doing just that.

Activity – Say Yes!

Today, let's play with possibilities and let go of the urge to predict the future. Start by asking your child (if you live with them) what they want to do today, and whatever it is (unless it's illegal or too dangerous), say yes. Your mind may groan and tell you that doing that won't be fun, that it's too hot, too cold, or that you should be working on something else. Do it anyway.

When you start the activity, act as if you had never done it before, never been there before, and take in every detail of the experience. Don't try to catalogue it mentally or cling to it, just experience it in the moment, then let it go. Feel the breath in your chest. Look with clarity, listen closely and notice what life is like when you embrace what *is*, instead of thinking about what could be better.

Continue with the activity for as long as you can, as long as you wish, or until something else takes over. Bring a spirit of play, of lightness to what you are doing and let the mind's judgements come and go as they please. They're no problem when you are present.

When my children ask me to play something that is messy, or that seems like a lot of work, I sometimes notice an internal groan, as if there's a boardroom in my head and that negative person who ruins every idea before it gets started is holding court. You know the one. They exist in our heads and in the world, and they know, before anything has even been started, why it's not a good idea.

I have noticed, though, that if I go with the idea, embrace it and jump in wholeheartedly, a few things happen. Firstly, the experience is a whole lot of fun for me and my children. Secondly, it often leads into unexpected, unplanned fun as the energy of what we are doing morphs into something else. And thirdly, I feel more alive, alert and present than if I resist the suggestions of my children, which are, after all, the flow of life.

Your children are more closely connected to the beginner's mind, to the simple fun of chasing a crazy idea, and contrary to popular opinion, it isn't your sole job to help them to be sensible. Sensible, in this context, is not sensible at all, it is deluded. You think and believe that you know how this will turn out, so you become resistant, you block it and you feel the suffering that goes with resistance. And all from a simple misunderstanding. You never know how things will turn out. In fact, nothing ever really turns out, because change continues moment after moment.

You never know where the possibilities will lead, but today, let them lead you.

Day 6: Knowing What to Do (Without Knowing Why)

With all this talk of the beginner's mind, of not knowing and of going with the flow, it may seem that we could never take decisive action as parents. It may seem, in fact, that we need to defer our responsibility for decision-making to our children. Not so.

This misconception is based on the belief that action is driven by thinking, that we must first think about doing something, then decide whether it is a good idea or not, and then either do it or not. It seems like this because we are so lost in thought that we are listening to a constant commentary that seems to be running the show. But, if you watch, the commentary is often behind, because the body acts without thinking in many cases.

While we may believe that we take action based on careful thought, in truth, much of what we do is a natural response to what the moment asks of us. The cold wind blows, and you zip up your jacket. Did you think about it? Did you weigh up the possibilities and write down a plan? No, you felt cold, and the body responded without thinking first. Then, when you meet your friend, you may tell the story of how you were so cold that you decided to zip up your jacket, but this is an illusion.

After you meet your friend, you might notice that words come out of your mouth before you have a chance to consider them. Sometimes thought precedes speech, but often words tumble out in response to what is being said or what is happening, without careful mental planning.

In fact, if you pay attention to the number of tasks in your life that actually require thinking, you may be surprised to discover that mostly they don't. When you learn a new skill or do some complex calculations, perhaps you need to think, but most of life is made up of small, simple tasks that can be done from *awareness* instead of from *thinking*.

Just now, I heard my son stir in the next room. He has a fever, and I found myself standing and walking to check on him without a first thought. I then found myself walking to the kitchen to get a glass of water, which I poured in clear awareness. I looked outside and saw the towels on the line, so I brought them in. There were thoughts floating in and out through all this, but I wasn't lost in them, and they didn't drive me to do those things. Of course, afterwards, I might say that I thought I should keep an eye on him, that I realised I was thirsty and spotted the towels on the line, but in real time, it wasn't like that, it just happened.

This way of acting and making decisions is incredibly simple. You do what is in front of you, without thinking about it. Often, people think about the task, about what they will do next, or they mentally complain about having to do it. Here is a simple way to escape from this mental water torture.

Activity – Non-thinking

Sit down for a moment and do nothing. Follow your breath, pay attention to your body and allow everything to be as it is. Sit in this way, watching thoughts come and go, experiencing emotions in the body, without an agenda, an aim or a destination. Sit and wait.

Stay there, not doing anything in particular, until life calls you to move. Maybe the phone rings, or the kettle sings, or the baby wakes. Whatever it is, take care of it, but as you do so, pay attention to what you are doing, not what your mind *says* about what you're doing. Be more interested in the experience than in the story.

Once you have answered that call from life, come back to your chair, unless the call leads on to something else, and wait. The next call may come from the world, or from your mind. You may remember that it's your aunt's birthday or that tonight is bin night. Your mind can remind you of things, but once you're committed, walk with your legs, not your mind. Feel with your hands, not your thoughts, and greet the world with your attention, not your opinions.

See if you can continue this practice throughout the day, unless you need to use thinking for some reason for a while. Otherwise, try to live through your body, through your experiences, not through stories and concepts.

When it comes to parenting, it is easy to get caught up in thinking things through and planning for the imagined future. In some ways, everything we do seems to be designed to achieve some future goal, like helping them to be successful, to grow well, to thrive. But true success arises from careful attention to detail, moment after moment. Great journeys are completed through thousands of tiny, careful steps. Being a truly successful parent means being completely present with your child, right this second. That is the only possible success. Everything else is a thought in your head, the story of a future.

Today, as you walk the journey of being a parent, be attentive to each step, and take care of what is needed this instant.

Day 7: Don't Know Anything

The unknown has a bad reputation among humans. In many ways, we prefer predictable unpleasantness to the complete unknown, because the ego is frightened of it. By ego, I mean your thought-created identity, your thinking mind when you are identified with it. This identity is petrified of the mysterious, and somehow drawn to it at the same time.

But if you look closely into your actual experience, you will find that, in fact, you don't know anything. It seems as if you *do* know, because you tell stories about what is happening and what will happen next, and often people agree with these stories. But they are stories nonetheless. You don't know if they're true or not.

For example, every weekday I ride my bike down the hill to work, and every day my mind tells me that I am going to work. It seems that I know I am going to work, but actually I have no idea what will happen in the next moment. Will I get hit by a car? Have a heart attack? Forget where I work? And can I even know for sure that I do have a job there? Maybe I'm dreaming, or hallucinating. Until the moment I am at work, I don't know, really, it's just an image in my head.

And the same goes for family. As I sit and type, it's me alone in the room. And although my mind says that my children are asleep in the next room, I can't really know, I can't prove it. I could stand up, walk in there and see for sure, but right this instant, I have no children, except in my mind. Without a story, it's just me, sitting, tapping on keys. Apparently that's for your benefit, as you will read this one day, but that's another story I can't prove as I sit here now.

This way of seeing the world may feel a little disconcerting. It might be uncomfortable or even confronting at first. After all, those stories give us a sense of predictability, of stability that makes the ego feel safe. But if you look around at the unpredictable nature of the universe you will quickly see that this is a false sense of security, because nothing is stable.

But let me be clear, we are not developing a new story in which 'nothing can be known' or 'the world is unstable'; we are stepping out of knowing (thought) and into not-knowing (experience). Try this activity for ten minutes today and you will see what I mean.

Activity – Not Knowing

Knowing in this context means being lost in thought, seeing the world through concepts, so let's start by moving attention out of thought and into the body with a couple of mindful breaths. Feel your body breathe in and out and allow your attention to move deeper into your body. Feel the sensations that are arising inside you, notice any tightness or tension, breathe and enjoy.

Don't allow stories to take over again. Keep returning your attention to the physical body and stay focused on what you feel, moment after moment.

Once your attention is in your body, go about your daily business, but see if you can be anchored in the body as you move, act and speak. Notice the mind's power as it grabs your attention again and again, and feel the difference between seeing the world through 'knowing' and experiencing it through awareness.

When you relate to your children and family members today, be present with your entire body. Experience the moment you are sharing with them fully and be wary of thoughts that arise and take your attention away. Get to know your loved ones through awareness, instead of through concepts, opinions and stories.

Being with children of all ages is wonderful because they won't kindly allow you to keep your stories intact. Children are masters at exposing the truth and putting stories under heavy stress if they contradict reality. So, if you are lost in thought and you are parenting, it is bound to be stressful, sooner or later. And when that stress arises, it can remind you to be here in your body instead. When you feel anxious, tense or upset, don't focus outwards and try to change your child. Use the emotion, pay attention to it and let it draw you back into the body, out of the story.

This is the in-built self-destruct mechanism that stress contains. When you suffer, you know to go inside, then the suffering stops, until you forget. When you forget to pay attention to now and go into story again, it hurts, and that can remind you to return to this. And so it continues. Being a parent amplifies this cycle, because you rarely get the rest that is possible when you are single or childless. As a parent, you can't unplug and do what you want for a day, you can't escape the demands of the day, and you often have another human to take care of.

So be thankful! You have the best job in the world to help you to become free of stressful thinking. Make good use of it and one day you'll be thanking your children for all those difficult moments.

Week 4: Key Learnings

- You don't need to be an authority figure, or to know everything, to be a good parent.
- Not knowing, but being curious to find out, is a far simpler and more effective way to live, and to parent.
- Step into this open, curious space whenever you feel stressed or disconnected from your children. Use the stress to uncover limiting beliefs and challenge old assumptions.
- Experiment with living with a little less certainty, and see what happens!

WEEK 5

Flow

Everything in nature either flows or it stagnates. Flow is a state of health, movement and energy. Stagnation leads to disease, staleness and problems. This basic principle applies to everything, from creeks and rivers to your digestive system, and everything in between. When energy moves smoothly, there is a delightful progress to life, a cycle that completes itself perfectly, and parenting is no different to any other process.

But before we explore how the practice of living in flow applies to parenting, let me explain it a little more clearly. Let's start with the breath, which is a great example of this principle in action. If you breathe in once, then stop, holding the air in your lungs, then you will die. Your body needs the in- and out-flow that it was designed to enjoy. And if the trees greedily soaked up the carbon dioxide without letting it flow back out as oxygen, no land animals could survive.

In the same way, if you cling to anything, be it money, food, relationships or beliefs, without letting it move on at the right time, things will be out of balance in your life.

As parents, and as people, we tend to get stuck, to cling in places and to try to keep things the way we like them, and this creates all sorts of havoc. This week, you will discover how to live in sync with life rather than resisting, dragging your feet and creating problems for yourself and others. And when you go with the current of life, it not only feels peaceful, but it tends to work out better as well!

Day 1: Teaching in Flow

As a parent, one of your important jobs is to help your children to live skilfully in this world. And, as discussed earlier, the best way to do this is to live skilfully yourself. But there are also times when you need to explain things, point things out and ask questions to help your children to reflect on what they are doing and find a more harmonious way to live.

The traditional parenting model for achieving this is to lecture, badger, remind and correct, using rewards, punishments (or call them consequences, if you like) and other tactics to achieve a controlled child. I say 'controlled' because all of these tactics rely on the guide being present. They don't teach children to figure things out for themselves. These methods also often bring about rebellion, especially in these times when children are highly tuned into any contradictions between what you say and what you do, even at a young age. Liam, my six-year-old son, is quite comfortable telling us that our tone is not very nice, or pointing out that we promised something yesterday and that we need to follow through. I don't remember being that switched on when I was six.

Even if these methods seem to 'work' on the surface for

some parents (that is, they bring obedience), they serve to put distance between you and your child, robbing you both of parenting's greatest gift.

Many parents know that they don't want to be the controlling ogre who keeps everyone in line, but they also want their children to be safe and to learn to be the best people they can. So, what to do?

The first thing is to continue to get in touch with your own true nature. Follow your breath, feel it and notice yourself as the awareness that is watching the breath come and go. That awareness is you, and it is inherently good. Everything we do that causes suffering, that is unskilful, comes when we get lost in thinking, without which we are naturally kind and compassionate.

Your child is the same, and if you help them to get in touch with that goodness, by sensing it in yourself, directing their attention to it and reminding them that it's there, even when they are not living from it, they will bring that goodness into the world. This doesn't mean they won't make mistakes, pull hair or forget to brush their teeth, but it does mean that those actions aren't who they are, they're opportunities to learn.

So your own mindfulness is the foundation. You need to know who you are, and to breathe through the difficulties that arise. If you lose your rag, you can't really help your child to learn, so start with that. You will notice that losing it usually happens when you get stuck and life keeps moving. You get stuck thinking about why something should be different, you anchor there and life keeps flowing around you. Floating in a fast-moving river is good fun, but standing still in one is very dangerous! As you hold your mental position, you create problems for yourself, and others may join in the drama.

They take an opposite view, telling you that you are wrong, and there is conflict and difficulty, and everyone is stuck. Life kept moving and no one noticed, so you're still arguing about that thing that happened yesterday, or last week, or in 1966. Whenever it was, it's gone. Learn from it and let go.

Once you are able to stay present in the midst of a challenge, you can see more clearly what is going on. You will start to notice details about what your child says or does in those situations, and out of that noticing will arise questions, observations or suggestions that are perfectly matched to the situation. Alternatively, nothing arises in terms of words or ideas, there is just the noticing. Then you will know that nothing is needed, merely the space for your child to learn for themselves. From this place of open, curious awareness it is much easier to see what may help most in this situation, and as you are completely open and curious, you can more easily join your child in a space of wondering. You no longer need to have the answer or the advice, you become the bringer of peace and space instead. It's a wonderful way to be.

Activity – Moving into Flow

Bring to mind a recent experience during which you got stuck in a particular thought, behaviour or point of view. Remember how the thoughts went around and around in your head, and how you became an immovable object in the world, unwilling to budge or compromise.

Remember, as vividly as you can, how it felt in your body when you were so rigid. It may have seemed that the situation caused that feeling, but in fact it was all happening

in you, which is much better news, because you can put an
end to it yourself.

Feel your breath in your chest and pay close attention to
what that is like. Feel the flow of it, and imagine how you
might have dealt with the same situation if you were in
your right mind, anchored in the moment. Picture the
scenario playing out, with you in flow, in sync with life.
What is it like?

A word of caution before we end today's practice: don't
turn flow into a goal or an expectation. If your mind succeeds
in turning this way of living into some sort of goal, then
each time you don't live up to this standard, it will feel like
a failure. And you will have times when you get stuck. The
important thing is to use it as a learning experience and move
on. Otherwise, you're stuck somewhere else.

Day 2: Learning to Flow

If you watch a young child in action, you will notice something
interesting: they switch smoothly and easily from one activity
to the next, all day long, without ever clinging to much of the
previous experience. Of course, we know that children learn
through these experiences, in fact, they are like sponges they
take so much in, but they rarely seem to get caught up in what
happened before in the way adults do.

For example, my three-year-old daughter Freya got very
grumpy with me today. She was given a little skateboard and

was learning to ride it on the carpet in the hallway. Freya is quite the daredevil, and would happily head straight to the downhill driveway for a spin, but that would be a bit much for us, so the hallway it was! As she was practising, holding my hand along the way, I gave her a suggestion, and she was not happy! She wanted to figure it out herself, and my suggestion ruined it. She started swinging fists of fury and kicking in that way that is only cute when you are three years old, and I decided to retreat and give her some space. Within less than ten minutes she had fully recovered, and we were back at it again, with no hard feelings (and no suggestions from me).

Let's unpack this a bit. I had done something that ruined her play. It was unintentional, but the result was devastating for her. I had taken over, wrecked her fun and then left when she got upset in the way that Bruce Lee used to do, and ten minutes later she was fine. As I sit here typing, I am imagining the conversation we would have if she were an adult (because adults tend to stew on things for much longer).

'Now, Dad, I need to talk to you.'

'Yes, Freya?'

'When you gave me that suggestion last week, it hurt me. I could tell that you didn't think I could do it by myself, that you don't trust me. I even stopped skating for a while because I lost my confidence. You've never trusted me, you're always taking over and I don't get to try things because you always think you know better. Why are you so controlling?'

We would normally say that the adult way is more 'sophisticated' and that children need to learn to deal with things 'like adults', but who has the real wisdom here? I learnt my lesson, Freya expressed herself and we moved on in ten minutes. She didn't cling to the past or project into the future and she was back enjoying life in a flash. As adults, we build complicated stories around simple misunderstandings, we tell others about them, we play around with those stories and we gain a sense of identity from our role in the stories. All this is complicated, time-consuming and energy-sapping, whereas Freya? She just flows.

Activity – Learning to Flow

I can't really learn how to flow like Freya, because learning is a process of addition, adding new ideas, concepts, thoughts and skills. On the contrary, I need to *unlearn* the habits that have become ingrained in me as an adult, I have to *unlearn* the process of anchoring.

Anchoring is the act of getting stuck, either at a point in time, or at a particular point of view. Eckhart Tolle calls this 'identifying with a mental position', which is a nice way of putting it. To anchor is to keep thinking about a particular thing in a particular way, even though life has moved on. Here are some ways to un-anchor yourself.

Bring to mind an anchor point in your life, which could be a belief, or a moment in time you keep thinking about. Pick something that affects your present moment experience, like a past hurt or upset, or a particular belief that clashes with reality.

As you hold that anchor point in mind, ask yourself these questions. Sit with each one in silence without trying to answer it, and see what arises:

- How does it feel to be stuck there?
- Is there any benefit to this anchor?

- What am I afraid of losing if I let it go?
- How would it feel to be here now, without it?
- What would others notice if that anchor came loose?

Take your time. Be patient with yourself as you contemplate each question. Then see what happens to that stickiness as you sit with those questions.

I learnt something amazing from Freya today. She didn't worry about teaching me a lesson, nor did she create a story about what my actions meant. In reality, they didn't mean anything, I just did them. She corrected me, trusted me to learn my own lesson, and moved on. And she had a ball in the process. She was focused on her own experience, and she skilfully kept out of mine.

Of course, she will probably learn in time to be more 'adult' in the way she handles these things, and then she'll get to unlearn like me. And of course hitting and kicking are not great ways to send a message, and she will learn to use words rather than fists, but I have to think that if I could use words as she used her fists – directly, in the moment and with precision – then I would have much less baggage in my mind, and much more energy and clarity.

Let the little ones around you teach you to flow and your life will change dramatically.

Day 3: Finding Where You're Stuck

Yesterday we explored how children can teach us to flow, and how we can pull up anchor when we're stuck in an uncomfortable mental position. Today we will expand that journey as we use the parenting experience to show us all of the places in which we are stuck. When you embrace these experiences and use them to get unstuck, by using what seemed like challenges as opportunities, life becomes peaceful as stress unravels by itself.

For me, the word 'stuck' implies that I am out of sync with life, which flows freely all around me. It also implies that I have lost touch with the present moment and moved into a state of resistance and unease as I think about what should be, instead of embracing what is. This happens all the time as a parent.

Tonight, for example, my son got very upset. He had a massive day and way too much sugar and by five thirty his brain was fried to perfection. He was getting angry at the drop of a hat and behaving like a six-year-old with a badly fried brain. Many times I have been in this situation, and many times I have reacted by trying to control, cajole or talk him out of it. And whenever this didn't work (which was almost always), I used the inner discomfort as a signal. Not a signal that something was wrong with him and that he needed to change (although that's what my mind was telling me), a signal that I was out of the present moment, that I had lost touch with myself.

Embracing stuckness as a signal, I went inside, time and again, to observe my inner state, to feel the discomfort and to see what thoughts I was clinging to. In the end, there were a couple of recurring themes, and they all started with the words 'he should'. But knowing that he is on *his* journey, I was confident that the answer to my own struggle lay within me. How ridiculous to blame someone else for my inner experience!

I used the following process to uncover the underlying stickiness, which helped me to move beyond it.

Activity – Finding Stuckness

Take a pen and a piece of paper and write the following:
I get stuck when . . .

Finish this sentence and see what comes out. For example:
I get stuck when Liam gets angry.

Next, write the following:
This happens because . . .

Take a moment to consider what drives the feeling. What story does your mind create around it? What does it say about you or the other person? How do you feel? Once you have a sentence that makes sense for you, write it down. Here is my example:
This happens because I believe that people should be nice to each other.

Take a look at what you wrote and consider it for a second. Take your time as you sit with what you have written.

This activity is interesting because we are making a shift in the source of the problem. Previously, it seemed as if the behaviour of the other person caused the stress, but now I know that it was my belief that clashed with life, making me feel uncomfortable. This means that next time you get stuck, you have the chance to remember that the stickiness is caused by what happens in your head, not by your experience at that moment. This is a very liberating realisation.

So, what do we do with stickiness, now that we have identified it? Personally, I use two approaches. First, I sit with it, fully experience it and allow it to be there. This takes me out of any resistance, out of any battle with my reaction, and allows me to make friends with it instead. The second tool I use is The Work of Byron Katie (www.thework.com), which provides a powerful, simple process for exploring, questioning and becoming enlightened to the beliefs of the mind.

Either way, as you sit still and notice the thought patterns that arise inside you and feel the emotions they create, you will gain clarity, insight and peace. It may feel uncomfortable at first to sit in this space, and your mind may want to move back into storytelling. The mind thrives on arguing with life, and it rarely gives up those arguments without a fight. But as you continue to practise sitting and noticing, you will find yourself less easily drawn into stories as you become more alert and aware. And as this ability deepens, you will find fewer and fewer problems in your life, and more and more opportunities to use stickiness to grow as a human being.

With these skills in your back pocket, you become free of stories, free to respond to the moment with clarity and peace, and your every action becomes a blessing for your friends and family. And then you forget, get mad, lose yourself in a story and make a fool of yourself. That's part of the process too, and is another opportunity to learn, so be patient, stay alert and enjoy the ups and downs of a life of mindfulness.

Day 4: When Love Flows Smoothly

When you are present, mindfully aware, there is a natural flow of energy from you to the world around you, including your children and family. Today we will explore how we can allow that natural flow to move freely into the world, and what to do when you feel blocked up.

Let's start with the most basic out-flow of energy – looking without labelling. When you look without mentally commentating on what you see (or at least without getting lost in the commentary that happens), awareness flows into that which you see. Sometimes I use the term 'pure awareness' to describe the act of looking without thinking about what you are observing, and although this makes it sound a little other-worldly, it is quite a concrete practice. Right now, take a mindful breath or two, and, as you do so, look at an object. Look and feel yourself breathing at the same time, leaving little room for your mind to chatter about the object. Notice the details, the colour, shape and texture of what you see, without needing to mentally catalogue those traits; just look. Make it more important to look carefully and closely than to understand.

This is pure awareness, and it is a profound practice in the family home, for a couple of simple reasons. First, your children need attention, but not only the kind we usually think about. Normally, attention consists of praise and blame, coaching and guidance and, sometimes, just being together.

This last class of attention is the most important, in my view. When we can share space without needing to guide, talk, comment or tell stories, we can listen to the other person. If you have ever felt truly listened to, truly understood and accepted without condition, you will know how wonderful this feels. In fact, it seems to be what every human craves, to be accepted as they are, and pure attention expresses this acceptance in a powerful way.

It is beyond acceptance actually, as acceptance implies that we have thought about the other person and decided that they're OK. This practice, on the other hand, involves looking without thinking at all. When this type of attention (which is the only true love) flows from you to your child, something amazing happens: not only do you allow them to be as they are, you also allow yourself to be you. And when this happens, you are able to give yourself what you always wanted from others: true, unconditional love. So, the second reason that this practice can be so powerful is that the awareness that flows to your child or loved one heals you too.

In practice, of course, this can be difficult to apply, especially when the kids are screaming, dinner is burning and the fridge is covered in red bills. So many external things seem to demand attention that it can be difficult to give it to our children, which is where this activity comes into its own . . .

Activity – Harnessing Attention

For a moment, let's picture attention as if it were a resource you could see and harness, like money. You know that you have a certain amount of money to use each week and you try hard, I am sure, to spend it wisely. Attention is similar. After all, you are awake for about 16 hours a day (maybe 18 or 20 if your kids are young), and so you have 16 hours of attention to give. Take out the time you spend taking care of the basics and you have even less time, and if you work or your child goes to school, or both, less still. Of course, you can be attentive during all activities, and I encourage you to be so, but the time spare for pure awareness may be pretty limited.

And what do we tend to do when these moments, these opportunities arise? We turn on the TV, or the radio, or pull out our phone. In doing this, we throw away our greatest resource: pure awareness.

Think of two or three things you regularly do that don't require your active participation in the usual way, like watching your child play sport, or listening to them tell you about their day. These are times when you don't need to think about what to do, times when you can just watch, listen and be.

Pick one of those activities and make it a focus this week to be as alert as you can during that time. Use breath awareness to anchor you in the present moment and look and listen without trying to figure out what is happening or why. Watch. Listen. Be.

Notice how it feels to be fully there with your child, and see how they respond. They may or may not notice, and either way is fine. This practice is for you, mostly, although they may benefit from it too. If your family are interested in mindfulness, invite them to spend five minutes together in silent awareness. If they're not, do it anyway. You'd be surprised how easy it is, most of the time, to sit silently as everyone else busily talks. I do it often and no one seems to notice!

Think of your attention as your most valuable resource this week, and see how you are spending it. As you do this, you may find yourself dropping or reducing certain activities, and doing others with greater awareness. Bringing this kind of open, curious attention to your children can rapidly change your world, and they may even come along for the ride. Be there with your children, enjoy their presence, and let them be exactly as they are, but only for this instant.

Day 5: The Flow of Play

We have spent a lot of time playing already during this journey, and with very good reason. Play is a present moment activity, which is why it is such fun! To play properly, you have to be there in the moment, watching, listening, paying attention. This is why even adults often love board games, cards and sport. It demands that you stop thinking about the problems your mind is creating and pay attention to what is, and this is tremendous fun.

Mostly, so far, we have explored ways that you can play with your children by joining in the games they enjoy or initiating something yourself, but today is a little different. Today it's all about you.

My friend Tiffany would like to play, but she doesn't have time. There is so much to organise, so much work to be done and the needs of small people to look after. And when that is done, she loses herself in social media, her attention sucked away into a virtual world until it is time for bed. This can get quite late, so in the morning, there's still no time, and not much energy either, so playing is forgotten.

I think this is quite common. People tell me that 'life is so busy these days', but when I ask what they do at night, they watch TV, they're on Facebook, or they're reading trashy novels. That's fine if you want to do it, but I wonder how much time there would be if the Facebook server went down for a week and the television broke. What would you do then?

Activity – Forgotten Games

What did you love to do, but now don't have time for? Take out a piece of paper and a pen and write down five things you used to love doing, even if it was 30 years ago. They don't have to be games in the traditional sense, they could be hobbies, or walking or exercising, or friends you love talking to. But pick things that you enjoyed for their own sake, not for future benefits, like better health or losing weight.

Make your list and then circle one, the one that you could do today, even with ten minutes spare.

Today, set aside ten minutes to do that activity, for its own sake. Don't set aside more or less, just ten minutes. If you go over time it doesn't matter, but don't set a massive time goal or it may start to feel like a chore.

When the time comes, bring your full attention to the activity. Notice how you feel inside, notice your breath, and pay careful attention to what you are doing. Be there fully.

Feel free to continue this playful practice for as many days as you like, and remember, you almost always have time for a play.

As a parent, it is easy to become serious and overburdened. It is also easy to zone out as soon as things get quiet. But to give your best to yourself and your children, you need a twinkle in your eye, a little bit of mischievous spark. And it is up to you to rediscover this if you feel it has been lost. Facebook won't do it, the TV won't do it; they only suck your attention and give very little in return. Discover your own playfulness and you will find yourself a completely different parent and person.

When I get lost in seriousness, lost in my head, it isn't pretty. Sometimes I think that my children must think an alien has wandered in and is impersonating Dad. I get snappy, grumpy, disorganised and muddled. This used to happen about once a month for a few days at a time (luckily this was before I had children), but now it lasts half an hour or so at the most. Still, I can feel the difference. My whole energy sinks, I become future-focused and I start trying to rush for no good reason. If you looked in my eyes in that moment you would see that there's nobody home.

And then I remember, the stress reminds me, that life doesn't need to be like this! Life is fun. I take a mindful breath and I smile. I look around and maybe crack a terrible joke. I stand up taller and breathe deeper. I'm back! I see my children smile or laugh, or yell or cry, and none of it matters that much. It's all a passing mood, a momentary happening, and I can deal with it as if life were a game. Some days you win, some days you lose, but it's a game just the same!

And although I am sure that my children like it better when I'm in the flow of playfulness, that isn't why I like to live that way. I try to live in this spirit because it feels right to me; it feels natural. So I do it for me, in complete selfishness, and my children seem to love it too, most of the time. Sometimes they're lost in their own stories, and that's OK, that's their journey. When I live in the moment, with a playful spirit for its own sake, then it doesn't matter what anyone else does, I'm responsible for what happens inside me.

If you want to live this way too, start with ten minutes. Then, simply notice the difference between those playful times and the hours on social media, or watching TV, or being a serious parent. When you feel the difference between those ways of living, you won't want to return to the way you used to be.

Day 6: One Thing at a Time

The concept of multitasking has become very popular in the last decade or so. You know the image: a young mum wipes a child's nose while cooking eggs and ironing, pausing to brush her teeth while buttering the toast and hanging out a load of washing. The idea behind this concept is that things get done faster if you do several at once, and also that intelligent people (especially intelligent women) should be able to juggle numerous simultaneous tasks. The reality is that humans don't concentrate or remember things nearly as well as we would like to think we do, and that switching between tasks, which is the only possibility as multitasking is not actually humanly possible, wastes a lot of time and mental energy.

As I sit here and type, there is only one task in front of me: writing these words. In fact, each keystroke is a task in and of itself. If I try to type a few words, then send an email, then do some dishes, then come back, the words won't flow in the same way. That flow comes from my undivided attention, which allows me to type with clarity and peace. The same is true for your life as a parent.

Aside from this, though, doing many things at once (or rapidly switching between them) leads to anxiety, stress and a chaotic environment. The opposite of this is to live like a Zen monk . . .

A disciple once asked the master, 'What is the essence of Zen?'

The master replied, 'Just do one thing at a time.'

You wake up in the morning. It's time to get ready for work and get the kids off to school. There are tasks to be done, and it's tempting to switch halfway through when you remember something else. Don't. Pick a task. They're all equal and they all need to be done before you leave. Choose one and do it, all the way through, with total attention. When you finish, move on to the next thing, then the next, until everything is ready. If you have time spare, spend it with your children or have a cup of tea, and do that fully too. Picture yourself flowing smoothly from here to there, with complete focus on what you are doing now.

Doing one thing at a time in this way has some surprising benefits. Because you can totally focus on this task without mentally jumping to the next, you will do things more skilfully, with better results. And as you will be able to do each task more mindfully, peace will flow into what you do, bringing a sense of calm into the house.

To do one thing at a time, though, you must learn to do without thinking too much. Jumping between tasks is caused by a simple split: your body is doing one thing while your attention is doing another. The body is cooking but the attention is thinking about eating the food. The body is still driving but the attention has already arrived. The antidote to this is to learn to go slow.

Activity – Go Slow

Have you ever heard of a 'go-slow'? It's a word that trades-people sometimes use in Australia to describe the act of deliberately slowing down your activity. The purpose of this may be different to ours, but we can learn to focus on one task at a time if we incorporate this little trick into daily life.

Think of a task you need to do today, something fairly straightforward, like washing the dishes or walking the dog. Before you start the task, take a moment to breathe and smile. Feel your body from the inside. Then, for the first 20 or 30 seconds of the task, go slow! Take your time, move slowly and enjoy the process. Be deliberate, careful and attentive.

After that slow start, keep doing the activity at the pace that feels right today. But keep your attention with your body – in the task, here and now. If it wanders ahead to some other moment in your imagination, come back to where the action is now.

You can expand this activity by simply taking a couple of mindful breaths before you start anything new. Sit in the car and breathe for a few seconds before you start the engine, listen to the phone ring twice before you pick up, or sit still at the table before you take your first bite of breakfast. You will be surprised how much a few moments of mindfulness, several times per day, can change your entire life.

Of course, your mind may be telling you that you don't have time to pause, to breathe, or to do one thing at a time. It may say that you're too busy! But don't take your mind's word for it, and don't take mine either. Run some experiments and find out for yourself. Does your morning routine take longer when you finish each task before moving on? Does your evening blow out because of a few mindful breaths before you start the dishes? And if things do move a little more slowly, is that a problem? We must remember that the human mind is always trying to get to the future, so faster always equals better, but what is the reality in your experience? Play with this practice this week and simply check whether you want to keep living in a busy, mad world or if you would rather step out of it, slow down and enjoy your life.

Day 7: Do What Arises

They say that failing to plan is planning to fail, and in many cases this rings true. If you are off to explore Antarctica for example, best you bring a map and some tucker, and in many other types of human activity a plan is needed to co-ordinate people, anticipate needs and to make sure you have what you need when you need it. But there are two elements to planning for most people: a practical element and a thinking, wondering, imagining element. Your mind tells you what to bring, but it also fantasises about what might happen when you get there, what could go wrong and what it will mean if you succeed.

On top of this, as we have seen, the mind is obsessed with the future. It sees its salvation as lying in wait in some future moment when everything has worked out, but this moment never comes! And so, we as humans have become obsessed with planning, with evaluating options, with figuring out the next thing. Watch your child and they can show you a different way to live.

My son Liam wants to play cricket. He begs and cajoles and, although it's 45 degrees in the shade and the concrete has turned into a frying pan, we head out to play. When we step outside, he remembers the lizard trap he was making yesterday, and our mission changes. Now my mind is geared up for cricket, it takes a moment to shift priorities, but I do so. We do some work on the trap and then a wasp flies past. We follow it (of course) in the hope of catching it, identifying it and having a look at its nest before a friendly release. Liam would like to keep everything as a pet but, of course, there are limits and wasps don't make the cut! After the release Liam hears the next door neighbour playing and soon he's over the fence, continuing on his way as he flows from moment to moment.

To the mind, this is wasteful. Nothing was completed, no games were played as planned and living in this way, the future is uncertain. Your mind values finishing things, putting them in rows, lining them up and knowing what comes next. If you have read A.A. Milne's classic books about Pooh Bear you will see that the mind is like Rabbit, while the spirit is like Pooh, wandering through and having a good time.

After all, in the end, when your life comes to a close, there will be things left incomplete. Bills will come in, there'll be food in the fridge, money in the bank, a cat in the living room. Your life will never be complete. So why strive so hard to get things done when you can enjoy yourself instead? Why push through tasks when there is fun to be had? Today I invite you to take a different approach.

Activity – Come What May

Set aside half an hour today to do whatever arises, whatever seems obvious. Don't plan in advance what you will do in this time and don't try to achieve anything through it, just do what comes. If it's sunny, you may find yourself going for a walk. If it's cold, you may find yourself bundled in front of the heater. But whatever you do, bring awareness and attention to it.

Follow your breath for a moment and as you do so, notice the gap that is there between breaths. Sit in that open spaciousness and just be, then allow the next breath to come.

Take this same attitude to what you do during this time. If nothing appears, just sit and be. Eventually something will present itself, and when it does, embrace it. When that activity finishes, there may be another space, followed by another activity, and so on. Keep doing what seems obvious with care and attention, and allow yourself to pause when there's nothing to do.

It seems to me that when I am lost in the imagined future my mind has created, I don't notice the things that the present moment is asking of me. The wasp flies by and I don't see it. The lizard trap sits there and I forget to keep building it. I have so many preconceived ideas running through my mind that it can be difficult to see what is right in front of me. Perhaps you know what this is like, to have an agenda that keeps the noticing at bay. Of course, we may not know that we're missing something, because in that state of mindlessness, we don't see it.

But when I am alert and aware, something magical happens. I notice opportunities that I would otherwise have missed. I see beauty, I find the humour in life and every moment is enjoyable. A lot of my life is like this nowadays, and the difference between the two ways of living is stark!

And the wonderful thing, the miraculous thing, is that I can still plan when I live this way. In fact, I plan more successfully, and I can adapt those plans moment after moment as life tells me what is needed next. This attention also allows me to see clearly what worked and what didn't, and it inspires new ideas for next time. Doing what arises, I am responsive, flexible, skilful and joyful, and there is no downside, whatever my mind may say.

Today you have a choice. Do you want to continue to strive towards a future that only exists in your mind? Or do you want to step into the flow of life and see what the world has in store for you this fine day?

Week 5: Key Learnings

- If you feel angry or stuck, use mindfulness to get back into flow before trying to sort the problem out.
- Bring awareness to your stuck points and they will naturally dissolve.
- Attention is a finite resource – what would you like to devote it to?
- Learn to do one thing at a time and to flow from one thing to the next. Your child knows how to do this – watch them and you will too!

WEEK 6

It's All About You

This week may challenge some of your beliefs and conditioning because the world has been lying to you about parenting. The world tells us, and we tell ourselves, that we're doing it for *them*, that we are doing things for our little ones, making sacrifices so that they can grow into the best versions of themselves. If you look at your actual experience though, you will find that everything that happens happens in you, *for you*. There is nothing outside of you.

Everything you see, hear, feel and think happens in you and in no one else. No other person on the planet has your experience, your life. So this week, as strange as it sounds, is about the supreme virtue of pure selfishness. It's pure because this selfishness is not the ordinary kind; it is a bit special. This selfishness doesn't involve thinking, scheming and planning; it can only be experienced and practised in the present moment, and it is the ultimate expression of love. This may sound like a paradox, but read on and you will see that the only way to contribute to your loved ones, and the world, is to be completely selfish.

The reason for this is quite simple: every time I do something for my children, it involves a story. How else would I know that I was doing it for them unless I was thinking about why I did it? Without the story, I would be responding to the needs of the moment, living out of my true nature, with no thought for the future, and when I live this way, I do it for me, because it feels natural and I love it. When I do something for my children, I am creating a future plan for them, thinking: 'If I do this then they will grow up to be kind and compassionate.' And when I put this expectation on them I am out of alignment with this instant, I am lost in my head. This is not true love, it is more like a bargaining process, a business agreement: 'If I do x, then you should reward me by becoming y.' This is unkind, as it tangles the other person in my agenda, which is none of their business. It is much kinder to live for me and leave those around me well alone.

This week, you will see how this applies, as well as having the chance to test it out in your own life. Keep an open mind, whatever your mind may say. The results may surprise you.

Day 1: Teaching For My Own Sake

The conventional way of thinking is that we teach our children how to be in the world 'for their own good'. It's not something we necessarily enjoy, but it's absolutely necessary, or so the thinking goes. This belief is built on a fundamentally flawed assumption that the future exists. I'm sorry to pull the rug if you were hoping that the future would be better than your present moment experience, but it won't. Worse than that, it's not coming at all. Sorry!

When we act as if the future does exist (which it *still* doesn't), we try to teach our children so that they can become functional adults, or grow and improve if they're adults already. This takes us into murky territory, where ends justify means, which meant that until recently, abusing children was seen as a good way to teach them to be kind, functional people. Huh? And whenever we need the imagined future to justify our actions now, it is probably because our actions aren't as kind, compassionate and considerate as we would like our children to become. So here's a question:

Does your child learn more from what you say or from what you do? Are they more likely to become kind and considerate if they experience kindness or manipulation?

Manipulation may seem a harsh word, but when I act in a certain way with the intent of making my children become something in particular, I feel manipulative. I'm not being transparent, I'm trying to mould them, I don't trust them to succeed as people without my meddling.

If I look into this behaviour and the thinking that underlies it, there is a common pattern: either I am hoping for a particular future or I am resisting something they are doing now. My son, for example, is a top-class whiner at times. He has that six-year-old's skill of hitting the right tone at the right cadence to make adults lose their minds. Mostly, I can sit with it, leave space for it, listen, and it passes. Sometimes, though, I tell him to stop it, I make demands, I want to leave the room. Why? I am resisting what is, and interestingly, when I do that, it lasts longer. The reason I tell him to stop (according to my mind), is that I want him to grow out of it, because otherwise he will have no friends and never get a job. When I leave space and allow it, I have a different motivation. I am prioritising my own peace, my own present moment experience, over any imagined future. I am being completely selfish.

To give up my own enjoyment, my own peace in this instant is foolish and it serves no one. When I fall into this trap, I am teaching my children that when someone does something you don't like, you should resist, argue, bully and control. And when they reflect that back, I don't like it! Reacting this way also puts their attention on me and my response, which reduces their opportunity for self-reflection. Allowing space for the noise to be there without my response clogging the airwaves, Liam can hear what it sounds like. In that moment, he's whingeing at himself, as well as me, and I trust that, when he hears it himself, he will want to do something differently. More importantly, I am leaving him in charge of his own journey.

Activity – Teaching Selfishly

Try this today in one or two situations: make your own inner experience your main responsibility. Don't worry so much about guiding others in the right direction, correcting their wrong ideas or making helpful suggestions. Focus on your inner world instead.

Take a few mindful breaths now and experience the simple joy of being present, here and now. Feel the peace that is there when your attention moves from thinking to the body. Soak it up and enjoy each breath in and out.

And when you are with other people, make it a priority to be mindful and enjoy your own inner experience as you interact with them. Make this your primary focus, simply being alert and aware, and let the other person be responsible for their own experience.

You can still guide if you need to, give information that may be missing or intervene to keep people (especially small ones) safe, but beyond this, be more interested in your breath and your body than you are in the future. Test this out in a few interactions today and see what happens.

When you live this seeming paradox – of selfishness being the greatest gift you can give – it reveals itself as a profound truth. The main contribution you make to the world around you is your state of being, so making your own peace more important than anything else allows you to give something beautiful – your presence. What you teach then is the art of skilful living, not through lectures or PowerPoint presentations, but through your very life. You become the model of kindness and compassion, and in my experience, an ounce of example is worth a tonne of explanation.

Day 2: Making Them Your Teachers

Yesterday we saw that by being skilfully selfish, you become a wonderful teacher through your very way of living. Today we will completely reverse the usual view of parenting by making your children *your* teachers.

Of course, we have touched on this practice throughout this journey, but today I want to take it a step further. Imagine, for a second, that the purpose of having children was to make you grow, develop and learn. Imagine that, instead of you being there to help your children succeed in this life, the roles were reversed; that the universe had sent them to your house to help you to find inner peace. Of course, having children may seem a strange thing to do in order to find inner peace, but stay with me! Your children push all your buttons, point out your faults, reflect back your delusions and demonstrate the problems with the way you live. What better teacher could you have?

Parenting is a bit like a Navy SEAL training course. The challenge shows up every chink in your armour and shows you when you are out of alignment with this instant. This 'out of alignment' looks like stress, fear, anger and all other forms of resistance, and it is a clear signal that we have lost touch with reality. Losing touch means that you are lost in your mind, imagining some past or future and projecting it on to the present moment. As we know, the past and the future don't exist as anything other than thoughts and images in the mind, but when we get caught up in those images, they can feel very real!

Your children can be great teachers, whether you want them to be or not, if you use the opportunities they provide skilfully, the depth of learning that can happen is quite breathtaking. And here is a simple, step-by-step method for making the most of every chance to learn from your children.

Activity – Bow to Your Sensei

When children behave in a way that your mind dislikes, or point out your flaws, or don't do what they are 'supposed' to, it is easy to get carried away on a stream of negative thinking. Here is what I try to do instead:

1 Notice that you are experiencing stress of some kind and realise that you are having a fight with reality.
2 Move your attention from your head (thought) to your body (experience) and feel that stress directly.
3 Stay with the direct experience of those sensations and if you get lost in the story again, come back to your body.
4 Allow those sensations to be as they are. Don't try to change or get rid of them, just feel them.
5 Repeat this practice every time one of your buttons gets pushed.

A few days ago, I experienced a great opportunity to put this into practice. I was in the kitchen, thinking about something else, when I heard fighting in the lounge. As I turned and walked in, I saw my two children locked in mortal combat over a book they both wanted (better than the TV remote, I suppose!). The stress was there instantaneously, as the behaviour I saw contradicted my mind's belief about how my children 'should' treat each other. I could have reacted, but instead I managed to separate them, and at the same time I directed my attention into my body, noticing the frustration that was arising. All of a sudden, I was in the present moment, whereas before I was daydreaming, and all because my kids gave me that opportunity!

Some Zen masters, even today, will give sleepy students a whack with a stick if they are slouching during meditation. This may seem cruel to us Westerners, but it is really an act of kindness. After all, what's the point of going all the way to a temple or Zen centre merely to daydream as you might at home? The master is like a personal trainer, pushing you to do better, even when you're tired and lacking motivation, although they're usually much cheaper!

My children play this same role in my life. Whenever I fall into a thought-dream, they're on me, asking for something, demanding something, or doing things I don't want them to do. This continually wakes me up out of thought, and it also reveals the buttons that can be hidden when you spend your days with fairly accommodating adults. Of course, they aren't doing this on purpose (at least I don't think they are), they're just being themselves! And I could easily become frustrated, upset and angry (and sometimes I do), and respond by trying to control them. If this control, which is the aim of many parenting books, was successful, my life might be more comfortable, and I could dream my way through it. But instead, I let my children remind me to wake up out of thought, and my mindfulness becomes deeper everyday.

I have done many retreats and sat with some incredible masters, but the little sensei in my house are my most effective teachers by far.

Day 3: Good Enough, For Now!

Thinking about parenting in the usual way, there is a real danger that you will become a perfectionist. Read some parenting blogs tonight and you will discover a different species of parent to you and me, and this idea is tempting to the mind. These parents are kind yet firm, they spend quality time with their kids, but always do the dishes and they are able to juggle the demands of a career, regular yoga practice and their role as ambassador to the UN, finishing each day's to-do list just in time to put the kids to bed and run their successful micro-business.

At my house, meanwhile, the kids are dirty and sometimes grumpy. The dog hasn't had a bath for months and the garden looks like it was modelled on the Gobi Desert. We forget the type of parents we want to be at least ten times a day and quite often our kids argue and have trouble getting along. Liam specialises in kung-fu moves in the lounge, while Freya is a master of the flying headbutt. Sometimes we're tired and usually we don't meet the standards of perfection set by our minds or by society.

Sometimes (usually when we're thinking too much), this seems like a problem, and maybe it feels that way for you too. At these times, my mind asks the question:

'Am I a good enough parent?'

Of course, to my mind, good enough means perfect, and as my mind compares the imagined past with its image of perfection, it is inevitable that there is a gap. It's a bit like comparing yourself with the models in those glossy magazines and aiming to look like them. The mind loves this process, because the gap between what is and what should be gives it a purpose, an identity and, most importantly, a future. As a parent, this may lead you to parenting books, blogs, Facebook quotes and advice from others, all in the hope that you can be perfect, one day.

This is a stressful way to live, and I prefer to ask myself a different question:

'Is this good enough, for now?'

It's not my job, actually, to do everything 'right' as a parent. It's not my job to be perfect. It's my job to do my best this instant, and this instant, and this instant. Knowing that what I do sometimes causes suffering for my children, I do my best not to do that again. But I also know that the difficulties I cause them can be a great blessing for them if they choose to work with those difficulties when they are older. I know this because my own journey down this path was started by the pain I felt, and at the time I thought other people had contributed to that. Of course, it was my thinking that caused the whole thing, but those people still helped me to start practising mindfulness, which has completely changed my life.

So it's possible that the problems I seem to cause for my children will be helpful to them. I still try not to cause the problems, but that's for me, as I'm a totally selfish parent, which you already know! I feel stressed when I act in ways that cause problems, and I prefer not to do that. And when I realise that I have made a mistake, I apologise, make it right if I can and am thankful that I have the opportunity to learn some more.

Activity – Good Enough, For Now

So what about you, are you good enough, for now? Let's take a look inside and see.

Close your eyes and take a few mindful breaths. As you do so, notice how every breath is exactly as deep or shallow as it is, without exception. If you had a mental concept of the 'right' way to breathe, this could be a problem, but without it, every breath is perfect itself. Simple.

Take attention into your body and notice what emotions are there, what tension exists in the muscles. Feel it all. Notice how your body feels right now, whether you allow it or resist it. And notice how, whatever is there, you can handle it, for now.

Notice what thoughts are passing through your mind and allow those to be as they are. Watch the mind and see that it is exactly as busy or as quiet as it is, and that this is also fine, for now.

And what about you? Breathing, feeling, watching thought. Are you good enough, for now?

The secret to this way of living is to deal with your present moment experience, unless there is an apology to be made or a plan to consider. Let go of the story of who you are as a parent (which comes from the past) and be aware of what is happening inside you this instant. You will notice that, without your story of perfection, you are a fine parent, right here and now. In this space of self-acceptance and simple joy, your children will love being around you, even though you might not always seem perfect.

Day 4: The Only Relationship

Today I want to explore something that may seem a little strange at first, but that can transform the way you experience the world: the realisation that the only relationship you really have is with this instant.

Of course, it appears that we have relationships with many people, and that those we have with our children are among the most important, but let's look at the observable facts. What we call a relationship is actually a series of thoughts based on what we see happening outside us. You see what looks like a person, they say things that your mind interprets as good or bad, and based on these experiences, a story develops about the relationship you have with that person. You call them 'my friend' or 'my enemy' and you make yourself happy or angry or whatever.

When it comes to parenting, these stories can be magnified as your mind tries to make an identity connected to the little (or big) people with whom you share your life. This includes evaluating the relationships you seem to have with your children and using these observations to label yourself as a 'good' or 'bad' parent, as well as commenting on whether you are close to your child or not.

In my experience, when I am not with them, my children, my wife, my friends and family members only exist as thoughts in my head, memories. I don't concern myself with whether they really exist or not; instead I experience my own life right now, in which it's just me. This morning, when my son woke me up, it was as if he was being born for the first time. Of course, I remembered him from yesterday, but the experience was so fresh, so new in that moment, that it seemed he had just appeared. One moment I was dreaming of something else, the next moment Liam appeared, ready to start the day.

And even when I am with my children, when I can see them, the only relationship I have is with this instant. When

I believe I am in a relationship with someone else, I am only relating to my story of them and my story of me. Without that story, there is merely an instantaneous interaction in which I fully experience this moment. To create the idea of relationship, I need to be thinking.

This may sound a little theoretical or philosophical, but look into your experience and see if it is true. When you think about your relationships, are they tangible and real, or do they come to you as thoughts, memories of the past? And are you ever truly in relationship with anything outside of the present moment? Try this and find out . . .

Activity – The Only Relationship

For a moment, set your stories of relationships aside and imagine that every person you ever met was a representative of the present moment. Picture them not as John or Jane, but as a part of your experience right now. Close your eyes as you do this.

Outside of your stories of those people, what do you notice as you close your eyes and remember these interactions? Are there sights, sounds and sensations coming to you right now? Your mind turned these into stories to make sense of the world around you, and to give a sense of continuity.

Drop the continuity too for a moment and keep your eyes closed. Follow your breath. Be still and notice. What do you still have a relationship with right now?

This doesn't mean that you will forget what your children are called, or that you won't remember to pick them up from school, but it does mean a possible shift in your primary focus. If your most important relationship is the one you have with your experience this instant, then many things become unnecessary. These include worrying about the future, about what others think of you, about whether your daughter really hates you, as she says she does. It also means that you can put your attention and your energy into taking care of your life right now, and leave others alone unless they need something from you. But this won't make you aloof and distant, as your mind may say, it will make you alert and calm, ready to respond to the needs of the moment, whether the moment comes as a purring cat, a happy husband or a crying child. If you appreciate and take care of your life right now, everything else will fall into place.

Day 5: Joyfully You

Amid the pressure, the demand and the busyness of modern parenting, it seems that many people have lost the joy of it. This can be especially true as children get older, answer back and get tattoos! As parents we can easily overburden ourselves with commitments and activities, and we can drown ourselves in stressful stories, leaving us tired, depleted and frustrated.

And many parents tell me that 'I don't get time for me', because they feel as if everything they do is for their children's benefit, or for their employer, their partner or somebody else. So today I want to share with you how I find time to enjoy myself, even when there is none.

The term 'joy' gives us a clue. While ordinarily we associate joy with particular activities, like playing sport, chatting with friends or drinking wine (or all three at once, perhaps), to enjoy yourself is to be in a state of joy that doesn't rely on anything outside of yourself.

As a parent, this is a very handy skill, because often having children reduces your opportunities to relax and do what you want to do. But what if you could switch into a state of enjoyment quickly and easily, with no preparation required and no time needed either? Here is how I manage this:

Activity – Enjoying Yourself

The first thing I do is to close my eyes and sit back in my chair. I feel the weight of my body against the back of the seat and I feel my breath coming and going. I become intensely focused on the breath as it comes in, then as it goes out I feel my shoulders, allowing them to drop and relax with the out-breath.

Try this for a few minutes now. Don't try to feel happy or joyful, just feel the in-breath and allow the body to relax during the out-breath. If there is stress or tension in your body, let it be there, smile at it and continue to breathe. Allow that smile to spread as the breath comes and goes and stay with that body awareness.

Congratulations, you are enjoying yourself!

Imagine how the world would change if everyone knew that all that's needed to enjoy yourself is to close your eyes and breathe! We wouldn't need so much entertainment, so much activity, so much to do, just plenty of tea and comfortable chairs. Your house can be the start of this. In fact, your inner world can be like this, even if the house is chaos! So much human activity is aimed at achieving something in the future that few people are able to enjoy their experience right now, but your life can be different.

Over the next few days, take a few minutes to enjoy yourself whenever you can. Once you get the hang of it, there is no need to be sitting nor to close your eyes. You can enjoy yourself in the supermarket, at the bank, on the train, anywhere really. And once you sink deep into this experience of enjoying yourself, you will realise that there are only two ways to live – in stress or in joy. Which will you choose?

As a parent, you may have full days and sleepless nights, you may be asked to do things for others many times a day. But even in the midst of this, you can enjoy yourself, you can breathe and be mindful, and in that you can change your entire life in an instant.

Be careful not to fill up your quiet moments with activity or distractions. It is easy to get in the habit of being busy, which can lead to an uncomfortable feeling during down times. So watch yourself carefully and notice when you are keeping busy for the sake of it. When you spot this happening, stop, sit down and enjoy yourself for a few minutes. You will feel the world slow down and the whole quality of your experience will change.

This way of living is not for the monks and mystics, it is for you and me, and it's available now. Slow down, sit still, and find the breath within your chest.

Day 6: For Your Own Sake

Today is all about those things we call chores, which is a dull and dreary word to be sure. In Western culture, chores are boring but necessary pieces of work that should be reduced, eliminated or at least done as quickly as possible. Even the word 'chores' may make you recoil a little, and the way we describe these everyday opportunities for happiness is telling. But what if you changed the way you approached these little moments of wonder and started to see them as they truly are – as another chance to bring attention into the present moment? Then, your relationship to your mundane, everyday life would quickly be turned upside down, in a good way.

In my worst moments, I don't hate chores, but I notice that I rush them. I power through, thinking about something else and wanting to get to the end. In that frame of mind, I treat these tasks as obstacles to my happiness. When I am at my best, I see them as a chance to express my happiness in a simple, concrete way. At these times, I do things for my own sake.

A few nights ago, I was doing my nightly writing. I write 1500 words a day most days, and so I sometimes put bills to be paid on the desk in front of the computer, as a reminder to pay them. But as I sat down and looked at them, the thought crossed my mind that 'I have to pay those bills' and I noticed a sense of unease, of pressure and of rebellion. This thought often comes when there is work to be done and it often leads to the procrastination of that work until tomorrow (which, of course, never comes). But as I sat with the discomfort of believing I had to do this task, something occurred to me: I like paying bills. Or, to be more accurate, I like to have things taken care of to the best of my ability. It feels right and natural to take care of those bills as soon as I can.

I feel the same way about the dishes. We don't have a dishwasher, so it's washing by hand morning and night. I don't think about doing the dishes, I notice them there, waiting, and out of that noticing, a response comes and I find myself turning on taps, scrubbing plates and doing the job with peace and contentment. I know deep down that I am not doing what 'has to' be done, I am doing what presents itself for my own sake. I am delighting in what the moment asks of me, rather than thinking about what else I could be doing or what to do next.

The truth is that anything you do is by choice. You are doing it for your own sake, because it seems right, or because it makes things better or whatever. You may tell a story that says you have to do it or someone is making you do it, but as you take the action and complete the task, you are always doing it for you, whether you notice that fact or not. You can either do that task with a head full of stress or a heart full of peace, and your way of approaching it makes all the difference.

Activity – Owning This Instant

Eckhart Tolle suggests in his book A New Earth that, whatever you need to do, act as if you chose it and see what happens. Today I invite you to take that a step further by imagining that you created this opportunity for your own development, and to embrace it wholeheartedly. Here's how:

Close your eyes and picture your least favourite daily chore, the one that needs to be done but is least enjoyable.

This might be a task, like washing the dishes, or a process, like driving the kids to school. As you picture yourself in that situation, notice what happens in your body, what arises in that moment and be mindful with that memory, so to speak.

Open your eyes and keep feeling your body sensations as you sit and read this. What is happening inside you?

Now imagine that you decided to challenge yourself to deepen your mindfulness practice in difficult situations by doing something you don't like every day. Picture yourself doing the task again, but seeing it as a mindfulness exercise, an opportunity to stay alert and aware in the midst of a challenge. What is the experience like when you take this attitude?

Every day, humans embrace unpleasant experiences because they are challenging, because they help us develop. We do this at the gym, at work and in relationships. Today, you can see what happens when you turn the experience you want to avoid into a chance to be mindful and notice what is happening inside you. At first, you may find yourself distracted and rushed, but keep coming back. Feel your body from the inside and see what you notice. As you do this, the challenge has reconnected you with the present moment, and all of a sudden those difficulties become blessings in disguise. What a wonderful way to live.

Day 7: Allow Yourself to Stop

When was the last time that you allowed yourself to do absolutely nothing, to step out of activity, even for a few minutes? Do you allow yourself to drop everything for a little while, or is there always something extra to do?

Activity, it seems, is the lifeblood of society, as well as a badge of honour. Doing something is seen as better than doing nothing, even though, if you look deeply, the vast majority of problems in the human world are caused by doing too much, not by inactivity. Especially in the West, we work harder than we need to, to earn more money than we need, to buy more things than we need. These things clog up our world, creating waste, using resources unnecessarily and leading to social inequality.

Excessive doing is closely connected to wanting, which drives all sorts of conflict and problems in this world. And in families, this can become the norm as well. A friend was telling me today that her eleven-year-old has to choose between music and sport because he has so many commitments in both. Hearing about these types of challenges, another friend, whose children are older, remarked to me, 'I'm so glad my kids were mediocre at sport!' Indeed.

This excessive activity leads to stress, anxiety and the inability to sit still without some external stimulation. This is an unbalanced way of living. In ancient cultures there are many examples of traditions in which people did nothing for long periods of time. In societies in which calories are scarce, it makes sense to take it easy when there is no need to do anything else.

In the West, we see this way of living as a little bit lazy, because we value activity over stillness, talking over listening, doing over waiting. But it is hard to argue that modern Western culture is the model way of living, as it seems we are creating many problems for ourselves and the world!

Instead, today, join me in a little bit of nothingness, which is more challenging than you might imagine . . .

Activity – Busy Doing Nothing

See if you can find 20 minutes free in your day to do absolutely nothing. If less is all that's possible, that's fine, but do your best to find 20. Sit in a comfortable position (this could be in your favourite chair, on the grass, against a tree or wherever you feel comfortable) and take your attention to your breath. Sit and observe the air coming and going from your body and allow yourself to sink into your chair.

Watch what your mind does. It may become restless, seeking something to think about, or wondering about all this wasted time. Stay with the process, and allow yourself the time to reset, the time to unwind.

Stay still, sitting in quiet stillness, for the time you planned. Stay with breath awareness and notice how the body starts to relax and rejuvenate through this stillness.

As a parent, the level of guilt about taking time to do nothing can be multiplied. After all, there is always something you could be doing to organise the house, arrange something for your family or get ready for tomorrow. And there is nothing wrong with any of these things, as long as they are balanced with enough space for quiet stillness. There is no need to not-do for 20 minutes a day every day, even a minute or two is sufficient.

As you get used to this process of slowing down, you may find something strange happening: you begin to feel as if you are doing nothing, even in the midst of activity. This has been my experience as I have continued to make space for stillness in my life. I do more and more things without thinking, so the body is active, but the mind is at rest. This is an incredibly calm and peaceful way to live, and it means that peace is infused into everything that I do.

And when I notice myself feeling stressed, I can always trace it back to too much thinking leading to too much activity and creating an imbalance. I start to feel tired, short-tempered and off-kilter, and I know that I need to stop. Then, a little bit of non-doing and I'm back in balance and ready to bring my best, most peaceful self out into the world.

Week 6: Key Learnings

- Your inner state is your first responsibility. Take care of it before you try to take care of anything else!
- Treat your child as your teacher, and thank them (silently) for every challenge they offer you.
- Forget about perfect and try 'good enough for now' instead!
- Your main relationship is with you. Enjoy yourself and use 'non-doing' to rebalance when you feel out of sync.

Conclusion

Over the past six weeks, we have been on quite a journey, and I hope that the trip has been rewarding, challenging and enlightening. But our travels together pale into insignificance when compared to the life-changing experience that is parenting. There is nothing quite so inspiring, scary, hilarious and confusing, sometimes all at once, and I hope that, in some small way, this book has opened up new ways of seeing your life as a parent.

Together, we have challenged cultural norms, exploded some myths and reimagined parenting, not in a quest for perfection but by taking the opportunity to grow mindfulness and presence in your life. In this way, every seeming failure, every challenge and everything you would rather avoid becomes an opportunity to grow and develop as a human being.

And so, as a parent and a person, you are already perfect, exactly as you are, seeming imperfections and all, and so are your children. As you keep walking the path, remember that in the mindful life there is no failure, and that in this instant there are no problems, whatever your mind may say.

Enjoy your journey, and keep in touch at oli@peacethroughmindfulness.com.au. I'm always delighted to receive questions, feedback and stories from the journey.

Thanks for being you.